WARWICK CAIRNS was born in Dagenham in 1962 and was educated at Keele and Yale universities. He lives in Windsor, England, with his wife and two daughters. This is his third book.

Also by Warwick Cairns

About the Size of It
How to Live Dangerously

WARWICK CAIRNS

In Praise of Savagery

FRIDAY
BOOKS

The Friday Project
An imprint of HarperCollins*Publishers*
77–85 Fulham Palace Road
Hammersmith
London W6 8JB

www.thefridayproject.co.uk
www.harpercollins.co.uk

This edition published by The Friday Project 2011
1

First published as an eBook by The Friday Project in 2010

A catalogue record for this book is available from the British Library

978-0-00-741403-1

Set in Minion by Palimpsest Book Production Ltd,
Falkirk, Stirlingshire

Printed and bound in Great Britain by
Clays Ltd, St Ives plc

Mixed Sources
Product group from well-managed
forests and other controlled sources
www.fsc.org Cert no. SW-COC-001806
© 1996 Forest Stewardship Council

FSC is a non-profit international organisation established
to promote the responsible management of the world's forests.
Products carrying the FSC label are independently certified
to assure consumers that they come from forests that are managed
to meet the social, economic and ecological needs
of present and future generations.

Find out more about HarperCollins and the environment at
www.harpercollins.co.uk/green

For Susan

Tho' it were ten thousand mile.

Yet they were a cheerful, happy people despite the incessant killing, and certainly not afflicted by the boredom which weighs so heavily today on our own young urban civilization.

Wilfred Thesiger, 1934

A Man Between Two Worlds

This was a man, you'll understand, who had killed – who had personally killed, as it were – so many people, over the years, that he'd lost count. Or rather, a man who'd killed so many people that he'd not even bothered to keep count in the first place. Not that he'd have been able to keep count, as it happens, even if he'd wanted to, what with the darkness, and the adrenaline-rush, and the pandemonium and the screaming, and the roar of the engines and all, and who could blame him for not keeping, for not being able to keep, an accurate tally?

Not me, I'm sure.

'What we did, you see,' he said, 'what we did was to park the Jeep. Park it behind a sand-dune or under some trees or bushes or scrub, if we found some, and then we'd cover it up with branches. Camouflage it, you understand. And then we'd wait.'

He eyed up my glass.

I'd not drunk anything yet.

'Cheers,' I said.

There was a sword hanging on the wall.

It was a golden sword, a great curved thing, sheathed in heavy gold, all carved and tooled and etched about, and encrusted with rubies and sapphires, and it hung from an elaborately wrought chain beside the fireplace. It was a bit of a monster, if the truth be told; like something that you'd see the pot-bellied genie carrying in an over-the-top am-dram production of *Ali Baba*, tucked into the sash holding up his pantaloons. And it is, I suppose, possible – just possible – that it was simply that: a theatrical prop, all gilt and paste, something that he'd picked up from a fancy-dress-hire shop on a whim, perhaps, as an amusing *quelque-chose*. Somehow I doubt it, though. He really wasn't the type.

I took a big sip from the glass.

'Delicious,' I said.

And, indeed, it would have been delicious, if I'd actually liked sherry in any shape or form. It would have been more than delicious, even, if I'd liked thick, dark 'cooking sherry' of the kind that your grandmother, perhaps, used to serve up to your parents at Christmas. But I didn't, as it happens, and don't, and never have.

It's not just sherry, either, but alcohol generally.

I don't know what it is about it, or about me, but I've never been able to get on with any of it. I just don't like the taste of it, I suppose. Sweet drinks I can sort of take, in small doses, liqueurs and the like, and advocaat; but even then I find myself wishing I'd had a glass of Coke or something, after a few sips.

'I've never been a great lover of Jeeps,' he continued, 'or any motor-car for that matter. The internal combustion engine has driven all of the silence out of the world.'

A clock ticked on the mantelpiece.

'It has brought nothing but noise and misery and dissatisfaction,' he said. 'I couldn't drive when I joined the Unit – did you know that? Couldn't drive at all. Didn't know where to put the key to start the engine. Didn't even know which way to turn a spanner to unscrew a wheel-nut. That amused the others no end. Now, with an animal – with a horse, say, or with a camel – well, you know where you are with them; and at least when they go wrong you can always eat them, if all else fails. But motorcars, no – they've never been my thing. But in the desert, when we found a camp we'd park our car, and hide it, and we'd wait until it got dark. And then we'd watch the lights in the tents until they went out, and we'd give them time to get off to sleep properly. Then, when it was all quiet, we'd jump into the car – me in the back with the machine-gun, driver up front, and we'd drive right through the middle of their camp and I'd blast away at the tents on both sides, and we'd be off before they knew what hit them.'

Shelley Court, Tite Street, Chelsea. The London home of Major Sir Wilfred Patrick Thesiger, KBE, DSO, honorary fellow of Magdalen College, Oxford, and holder of the Star of Ethiopia (Third Class).

He was a mountain of a man, Thesiger, even then, for all his eighty years, in his antique tweed three-piece suit with his pocket-watch on a chain and his handmade shoes; and he was a man who, in his lifetime, had done and seen extraordinary things.

In the dying days of the age when there were still blank spaces on the world's maps, and when there were still places from which no traveller had ever returned, he had set off into unexplored lands and crossed the territories of savage and murderous tribes, against all advice and in defiance of all reasonable expectation of survival, and yet he had lived to tell the tale.

In the years of war, he had led the small battalion that captured the Italian garrison of Agibar and all its 2,500 troops; and later, with the SAS in the Western Desert, when almost all of his unit had been captured or killed, he had gone in pursuit of Rommel's Afrika Korps, tanks and all, and had narrowly escaped being captured by the Field-Marshal himself.

In the years after, when others went back to their lives and families, he had sought out wild and comfortless places, living and travelling with the Bedouin of Arabia, with whom he crossed the 'uncrossable' sands of the *Rub' al Khali,* or Empty Quarter, hovering on the brink of death from lack of food and water.

And there was more besides.

Shelley Court lay at the end of a row of black iron railings, where four stone steps led me up from Tite Street to the heavy black-painted door of the red-brick mansion block, where I pressed a button and announced myself into the intercom, and heard, a few seconds later, the electric buzz as the lock clicked open.

Inside, I found myself in a small, bare hallway – little more than a stairwell, with a rattling wire-cage lift with a concertina-door running up the middle.

I took the stairs.

He was waiting at the top for me.

I tried not to look out of breath.

'Mr Cairns?'

He held out a bear-sized hand to shake.

'So pleased to see you. Do come in.'

The flat was crammed with books. Books filled the shelves, were stacked on chairs and tables, stood in piles on the floor. And on the wall hung a painting of himself – himself as a much younger man. And although much had changed in the intervening sixty years, the deterioration that comes to us all, in time, it was still the same man looking out – still the same strong jaw, the same distinctive, misshapen nose, broken twice in the days when he boxed for Oxford, and the eyes – the same, same eyes.

He turned.

'Did you go to Eton?'

'No, sir, I didn't.'

I didn't, as it happens. And I didn't think he would have been too familiar with the various comprehensive establishments of the

London Borough of Barking and Dagenham, where I did go to school, so I didn't elucidate further.

'Do take a seat. You can move those books onto the table there.'

I did.

'Now, can I get you a drink? A glass of sherry, perhaps?'

'Yes, sir, a sherry would be perfect.'

He left the room, and came back into it holding a heavy brown bottle and a glass – a single, large glass – and he placed them on the small table between us, and sat down in his chair. He still had on his jacket, brown herringbone tweed with worn leather buttons, although it was warm indoors; he reached into his breast-pocket and pulled out a blue-and-white spotted handkerchief, with which he wiped the dust from the sherry bottle before uncorking it. Then with a steady hand – surprisingly steady, given his age – he poured out the sherry, and kept on pouring, until the glass was more or less full to the brim. It was, as I say, a large glass, and it held about half a pint, or thereabouts, and he slid it across the table towards me.

'Thank you,' I said. 'You're very kind.'

He nodded.

'I hope you don't mind if I don't join you,' he said. 'You see, I can't bear the stuff.'

Nor could he ever.

Once, out hunting in the English countryside as a young man, he was handed a flask, from which he had his first taste of beer.

'It was revolting,' he said, 'I spat it into a hedge.'

And that, pretty much, was that, as far as his relationship with drink went.

I remember little of the detail now of what followed, except for disjointed snatches of conversation and images of long ago and far away. A young man's journey into a forbidden kingdom, on a quest to find the unknown destination of a distant river. A midnight meeting in a forest clearing with a savage potentate and his armed warriors, and the glint of curved daggers in the moon's pale light. The burning heat of desert sands. Wave upon wave of armed and bloodied hosts screaming out their victorious deeds before an emperor's throne. A great feast celebrating the killing of four unknown men – shot in the back and from a distance, for all anyone knew – and the young killer all shy and manful, he said, as praise was heaped upon him, like an athlete at Oxford being awarded his Blue for cricket.

Oh, and Salman Rushdie, and what an infernal bloody nuisance the man was, and the sooner the Iranians finished him off, the better it would be for all concerned.

I came out onto the street an hour later, leaving behind an empty glass, and with an invitation to call again. Whatever I had said, it must, I think, have found favour. This time the invitation was not to Tite Street but to his other home, where he spent the majority of his year. This home, the other home, was a mud hut, and it was in Africa.

From Tite Street I followed the crowds on the King's Road, past the plate-glass shop-fronts, past the restaurants, past the antique dealers, the interior designers, the clothes designers, the cavalry barracks and the crocodiles of uniformed schoolchildren in their corduroy knickerbockers, and thence to Sloane Square underground station, where, down on the platform, a river flows above your head. I say a river, but it's more of a stream, a brook or burn that flows in from the west, and which is called the Westbourne. You can't actually see the water in it, or touch it, but you can hear it as it crosses above you, suspended, as it is, from the girders in a big old riveted cast-iron pipe, on its way out under the concrete and tarmac of the streets, on beneath the grounds of the Chelsea Hospital and then out from a Victorian outlet-pipe known as the

Ranelagh Sewer into the Thames, the great brown river whose ancient name, like that of the Tame, the Teme and the Tamar, meaning, perhaps, 'the dark one', goes back far beyond recorded history.

But as for the Westbourne, there was a time, once, when it was a real stream, a stream with grassy banks and trees leaning over it, and when it crossed open land – fields and forests – as it flowed from its springs in the Bagshot sand in Hampstead down to the big river. The Saxons called it the Cy Bourne, or King's Burn: over the years that became 'Kilburn'; in other times it became the Serpentine, which it still is, briefly, in the short space where it comes to the surface as an ornamental lake in Hyde Park. Mostly, though, it has been lost and forgotten, along with all the other lost and forgotten rivers with which London once teemed – the Tyburn, the Fleet, the Walbrook, the Effra, the Wandle, the Peck, the Ravensbourne . . . It lives on today only in the street-names and place-names of the areas through which it once passed.

Does drinking too much sherry when you're unaccustomed to it make you think about things like this? 'Maudlin' is the word that comes to mind here, as I write these words: yes, maudlin – that's it. I can't say that I'm a great expert in these matters, but I thought, the world moves on and by and large we're all the better for it. And yet . . .

I didn't know what, precisely, but 'and yet something' was definitely a part of it, if you get my drift. There was a definite 'and yet' in there – still is, in fact.

Where I come from we have cars and things, and shopping, and we have computers and televisions and bars of chocolate – we have all sorts. No one starves here – which is good. And that was not always the case.

But sometimes you catch a glimpse of what things were once like, and you have intimations of what went before, and of the other lives and times of the ground beneath your feet. And it makes you think, and it makes you wonder what the cost has been, what the price paid, in getting to where we now are.

The economist Milton Friedman once said that there is no such thing as a free lunch. With civilisation, with the way we live now, with all of the things we have, what we have is not so much a lunch – free or otherwise – as a massive multi-course banquet of extraordinary proportions, a spread wholly unimaginable to previous generations.

Imagine what your great-grandfather would have thought, to be here now; imagine what he might have said, to see what you have and where you live, and what you do. Or imagine your great-great-grandfather, more to the point, or all the generations before, all the way back to the woad-painted wattle-and-daub-hut-dwellers we came from. Imagine if they could be lifted out of their time, just for the day, and set down in the middle of your life now.

There is a story that back in the 1940s the Soviet Union bought the film of John Steinbeck's *The Grapes of Wrath* to use as propaganda, to show how bad things were in the 'free world'. Steinbeck's story is, as stories go, a pretty miserable one, with the Joad family, like many others in that place at that time, losing everything when the rains fail and the rivers run dry and their lands turn to dust, and the daughter burdened with the ridiculous name of 'Rosasharn' and them being forced to load up onto their battered old car what few worldly possessions they have and set off to try – spectacularly unsuccessfully – to find a better life elsewhere. Everywhere they turn they are shunned and insulted, and doors are slammed in their faces. And people die. It doesn't get much worse than that, you might think. But when Soviet audiences saw the film, they didn't see the same things that you or I might see, and they came out shaking their heads in wonder. They came out shaking their heads in wonder not so much at how bad things were in the USA, but at the fact that over there even the *poor*, even the lowest of the low, even peasants driven from their farms, that these people had their own motor-cars. Their *own*. The film was subsequently banned.

That's what civilisation is like, these days. Even the poor people have motor-cars, now, and computer-game consoles, and new clothes, and more food than they need. Even the poor people are getting fat. A bit of starvation would probably do some of us quite a lot of good, you might think – and not just the poor, either, to look at our expanding waistlines.

But as you surfeit on the sumptuousness of it all, this life that civilisation has served up, and the feast that's spread out for you, you might find your mind wandering, from time to time, to the issue of the bill, and to what extent you, personally, will be expected to pay.

You might begin to wonder what the damage is here, exactly. Or is there none? Do we genuinely have, this time, if not a completely free lunch, then at least a damn cheap and filling and tasty one? And Wilfred Thesiger, explorer, nomad, ex-Eton and Oxford and His Majesty's Colonial Service, distinguished SAS officer and sometime military adviser to Haile Selassie, wanderer through the lost worlds of vanished tribes, current resident of Tite Street, Chelsea, and also of a mud hut in the middle of nowhere, was probably as good a person to ask as any.

I booked my ticket the next day.

Cheques and Balances

Go back a couple of years, and you will find me behind the counter in a provincial high-street bank, lending money to people. Go back further still and you'll find me upstairs in that same bank, in what was known as the 'machine room', taking the elastic bands off bundles of cheques and then counting those cheques, sorting them into account-number order and walking up and down the great long tables that dominated the room and stacking the cheques onto the appropriate numbered sections, for some eight hours a day.

There were machines there, also: quite big ones, I seem to think, but I can't for the life of me remember what it was that they did. Perhaps I never knew.

You get faster at it, after a while, machine-room work. And you could go up to people who'd been there a long time, give them a block of cheques and say, 'count those', and they'd tap the block against the table once or twice to square the edges off, set it down, flex their fingers and then there'd be a blur of fingers and a whirring of paper, and half a second later, or whatever it was, it would be 'a hundred and twenty-seven'. I am convinced that some of the tapping and the finger-flexing wasn't strictly necessary, but was a vanity, an affectation, to impress, a little stylistic flourish to say, 'Behold! Here is a master of the art.'

These skills, such as they were, and to the extent that I mastered them, did not transfer well to lending money to people. Lending money to people was something that I did worse than I did counting cheques.

People would come in with the most outrageous stories of why they needed money and, most times, so long as they managed to keep a straight look on their face and a credible tone to their voice, I would believe them.

'I need,' said one woman, 'a completely new wardrobe.'

'But you have no money. You have, in fact, less than no money. And this has been going on for . . . well, it looks like several years now, as far as I can see from your file. We need to talk about how you intend to pay some of it back, rather than how much more of it you need to borrow.'

'Well, that's why I need this money, you see. You see, what it is, is that I've just been offered a job. And it's a good job, a proper job in an office – but the thing is, I don't actually have any office clothes to wear, other than what I've got on, which is what I wore for the interview. So I need the clothes for the job, to earn the money to pay back what I owe.'

'Oh, I see. Well, that sort of makes sense, I think. How much is it that you say you need, for these clothes . . .? I'm sorry, *how* much? Really? Well, that does seem a bit steep . . . No, I do know how important it is to create the right impression. And as you say, it will give you the ability to pay back what you owe. I'll just get the paperwork sorted out. You'll need to sign here . . . and here, too.'

She was glad that I understood these things, she said, as she signed. Not like her mother, who'd advised her to make do with what she had. Not, of course, that she actually had anything to make do with, as she'd already explained.

I never saw her again, or the money, either.

12

And all the while and all the day in my peripheral vision and hearing – and sometimes more directly – I could see, and hear, and feel the under-manager, who ran the day-to-day business of the bank, and the rising sense of stress and panic with which he started and finished every day of his working life. That deadlines should be met, that queues should not be too long, that people should not take much time over their tea-breaks, that people should arrive in the mornings precisely when they were meant to arrive (and on the dot of nine, the signing-in book was whisked away to the manager's office, whence anyone whom arrived after should go to explain themselves), that procedures should be followed, that shoes should be shined and trousers pressed, that the books should balance. All these things concerned him greatly, and visibly and audibly. As each day wore on, the note of tension in his voice would grow more strangulated, the temper sharper and more hair-triggered, and for every fault or omission he spotted and corrected, others would arise, hydra-like, to take their place. Too many humans in the machine room of his bank; too much slackness, too much imperfection. Fraud and deception.

You would get the ones who planned it all in advance. People who'd open an account – sometimes in their own name, or sometimes, on some pretext, with a friend or colleague, with whom they'd sign the mandatory declaration of 'joint and several liability' making them both personally liable for all debts on the account, whoever caused them.

They'd keep the account ticking over, quietly and in credit, for a year or more, putting in requests for a new cheque-book every now and then, until they were good and ready, when, all of a sudden, there'd be twenty cheques issued in a single day, and more the next, and the next, and they'd be drawn out to off-licences and clothes shops and casinos, and the account would go tens, hundreds and thousands of pounds overdrawn in the space of a single week. You'd phone the account holder, send letters, but there would be no reply. And so you'd bounce the cheques, and brace yourself for the wave of angry phone calls from outraged creditors and even-more-outraged co-account holders.

There was a correct response to these calls, which was, 'I'm very sorry sir/madam, but I am not at liberty to discuss this person's account. Or their whereabouts, I'm afraid', to which I'd add sometimes that the address I really, really wasn't allowed to tell them was number 11, Ferndene; or that the phone number that I was not, unfortunately, at liberty to divulge, might have been 673562, if I'd been allowed to say so, but since I wasn't, they'd have to look elsewhere to find it out. That tended to stir things up a bit, I found. Particularly if the voice at the end of the line sounded like someone who intended to take the matter somewhat further to recover their money.

'Golf,' said the under-manager.

'I'm sorry?'

I think I must have drifted off somewhere, off into my thoughts. I had a tendency to do that. I have a tendency to do it still. I was, I think, sitting at the foreign exchange till at the time. It was a quiet afternoon, on a hot summer's day, and there were no customers in that section, had been none for a while.

'Golf,' he said. 'Do you play it?'

'Er . . . no. Not exactly. It's not something I've got round to doing yet.'

'Oh,' he said. 'Well, never mind. There are plenty of people who've managed to go quite a long way in banking without ever playing golf. Now, your suit . . .'

'My suit?'

'Ye-es. Your suit. What's it made of?'

'I'll have to have a look.'

The label said 75 per cent cotton, 25 per cent linen. I'd bought it for the weather, for the summer.

'I thought so,' he said. 'Disco suit. Don't wear it again.'

In the backrooms there were fans on the desks, beige oscillating fans that swayed from side to side and caught the stray unweighted papers of the unsuspecting, lifting them up and sending them seesawing gently down to the worn brown carpet.

In the restroom where we took our morning and afternoon tea-breaks there were no fans, but there we were allowed to remove our jackets and to roll up our sleeves.

Brian, a middle-aged clerk with a close-cropped sandy beard, never rolled up his sleeves, no matter how hot or still the air in the restroom. He was a middle-ranking clerk, quite old for his position, and he had been at the same level for many years now, far longer than most. I was never quite sure whether it was for golf reasons or for the quality or fabric of his suitage or for some other cause that he had never progressed, but he had not done so, nor did it seem to bother him, particularly.

One day we were sitting together in the restroom sipping vending-machine coffee from plastic cups when I asked him about his sleeves and why he never rolled them up.

'Do you really want to know?' he said.

I said that I did; and with this he put down his cup and beckoned me to follow him outside, into the corridor. There, after checking in both directions, he undid both cuff-buttons; then, looking me in the eye, he pulled back first one sleeve and then the other.

'There,' he said. 'What do you think?'

His arms, both of them, right down to the wrist, were covered, with barely a patch of flesh to spare, in blue-green tattoos. Mostly they were of skulls and motorcycles, and skulls in Second World War-German-Army-style motorcycle helmets, and motorcyclists with fleshless skulls for heads. There were also the logos of the old British motorcycle manufacturers surmounted by skulls, or just in the general vicinity of skulls. And, on one arm, a naked lady wreathed in a large snake.

'Gosh!' I said, or words to that effect.

'I'm a Hell's Angel,' he said.

And thereafter he would tell me, when we were alone together, about his weekends with the Chapter, and about motorcycles and how to customise them to make them just so, and why, when a big petrol tank meant that you could ride for longer and make fewer stops, it was a good thing to replace it with a smaller one, from the point of view of just looking hardcore.

All of which made sense to me then and seemed only right and natural.

I was twenty-three years old, or thereabouts. I saw the world of work, then, as what people had to go through, to pay for what they wanted to do in their 'real' time, the time that mattered. And all the business reports on the television talking about the FT-100 Share Index and whatnot, and the copies of the *Financial Times* in the newsagents, and in the bookshops the shelves upon shelves of books with titles like *Odyssey: From Pepsi to Apple*, *The Ten Habits of Successful Business Leaders* and *The Corporate Warrior: Your Road Map to Success*, I thought, then, that they were what people had to read because of their jobs, and what they had to put themselves through to earn their living. But that beyond these, I thought there were other things that meant more to them: I don't know – golf, say, even, or motorcycles, or tennis or something. Now, I don't know so much. Now, I'm not so sure. There are people, I have seen, who every day when lunchtime comes, stay at their desks. There are people who, every day when home-time comes, don't go home, but instead stay on at work for hours. There are people who, though they have holiday allocation, don't take it all, or even much more than a fraction of it; and who, when they do leave the office, take with them the concerns of their company, take them on as their own and carry their work around in their heads with them, and when they talk, they talk about work, or else they constantly check mobile electronic devices for messages to do with work. There are people who earn the most extraordinary sums of money working in offices, but who do not know what their own children like to eat. There are television programmes about work, too, game-shows in which the contestants vie to be the best shopkeeper or salesman or distributor or wholesaler, and for whom the prize, should they win, is a job in an office in a provincial retail park.

I shared a taxi, years later, with a businesswoman I had been working with, a senior executive with a multinational company who had lived, for a year or two at a time, in more countries than she could remember, who regularly attended breakfast meetings before work and evening functions with business colleagues and contacts after work, and who said goodnight to her children, most nights, by telephone as the nanny tucked them in; and as we drove, by way of conversation, I asked about her husband and what he did.

'He's an entrepreneur,' she said.

And indeed he seemed to be a successful one, for between them they had an expensive house in a sought-after part of London and a second home elsewhere, and several expensive cars. They both had their clothes made for them by tailors, and had all of the things and did all of the things that successful people have and do.

'And what are his hobbies?' I asked.

It took her a moment or two to make sense of what I had said. It seemed to be not the sort of question that she was used to being asked by the kinds of people she habitually mixed with.

'Business is his hobby,' she replied, at length.

'But outside business? I mean, does he have a sport he likes, or an interest or something?'

She thought again.

'I asked him once. I said, what would you do if you couldn't work? If you'd earned so much money you didn't need to. And he said, "I'd start a new company".'

For some people, work is the thing, the main thing in life. Work is what they choose to do and where they want to be. Work is life.

But at that time I did not believe this to be so.

Sultan of Aussa

To the east of Abyssinia there lies a desolate volcanic plain, strewn with ash and tumbled black rocks, almost entirely empty of life and swept constantly by a burning salt wind. What vegetation there is grows close to the banks of the slow-flowing, mud-red Awash River, which winds its way down from the mountains, down through deep gorges and into the barren desert, where live the people known as the Danakil, who were, at one time, a murderous tribe split into two great bands, the *Adoimara*, or White Men, and the *Asaimara*, or Red Men. Among these Danakil, both Adoimara and Asaimara, a man's status was judged, entirely, by the number of men, women and children he had killed. This he might do by any means he pleased, no matter how treacherous. When they were not killing outsiders, or engaging in feuds with surrounding tribes, the two bands of the Danakil expended their time and their energies on killing each other.

The river flows on and on through the Danakil lands for mile after mile until there rises, in the distance, a line of purple hills known as the Magenta Mountains. There is a steep and narrow pass in these mountains, and the river flows through it, pouring down into an extraordinary oasis, shut in all round by sheer precipices of black rock. Some thirty miles square, it is a place of thick forest, deep swamp and huge lakes.

This is the land of Aussa, and it was, in the 1930s, the home of a great Danakil army who owed their absolute loyalty to the Sultan of that place, whose palace lay deep within the forest.

The Sultan, in those days, was a small, intense-eyed man called Muhammad Yuya. His father, the Sultan before him, had on his deathbed called for two slaves to be brought before him, one male and one female; and he had had them both slaughtered there, in the hope of seeing, in their death-agonies, some clue or portent that might help him escape his predicament. He could not. But no doubt it passed the time.

The river flows around Aussa on three sides, looking for a way out into the desert land beyond, where at some further point, before reaching the coast at Djibouti, it disappears. No one outside Aussa ever knew where it went.

There had been attempts to discover the river's destination, over the years; and over the years there had been a number of expeditions to Aussa, but none had ever returned alive.

An expedition, in 1875, led by the Swiss explorer and mercenary Werner Munzinger, accompanied by his wife and children, were all murdered before reaching the borders of Aussa. In 1881, two Italians, Giuseppe Giulietti and Ettore Biglieri, had mounted an expedition to cross the country to the north of Aussa to establish a new trade route. Their bodies were found lying in the desert, horribly mutilated. Three years later, fourteen armed Italian sailors had tried to cross the same land from the opposite direction. They, likewise, were all killed. And in the 1920s, a party led by two Greek animal-collectors was hacked to death, although a third Greek managed to escape, crawling away on his hands and knees in the brief space between being left for dead and the corpse-mutilators getting down to their work.

In 1933, at the age of twenty-three and not long down from Oxford, Wilfred Thesiger made a decision.

'I will bloody well go and do it myself,' he said.

Harlow New Town

It was, as houses on the outskirts of Harlow New Town go, a fairly normal one.

It was semi-detached, and vaguely modern in style; or what would have been considered modern sometime in the mid-1960s, when it was built. It had large double-glazed picture windows with brown frames, and a bit of dark vertical wood-cladding in some parts and off-white render in others, and it sat in a row of houses that were identical – or that would have been identical at one time, before the replacement-window and flat-roof-extension salesmen came around. Also the stone-cladding salesmen, for one of the houses nearby had pinkish and yellowish crazy-paving up its walls, for reasons best known to its owner, and also to the owners of other similar houses I had passed on the way. It was in a cul-de-sac, the house, a cul-de-sac with only half a name. I say half a name, but it was a whole name – 'Winchester' or 'Gatefield' or something – but it was a name without a description – it wasn't Winchester *Road* or Gatefield *Close* or whatever – it was just what it was without the attachment. Things were like that, round that way, when they built Harlow New Town. It was a time when people knew better, you see.

21

The end of the Second World War – the cities bombed to smithereens, the population subsisting on powdered egg and dripping, the biggest and most powerful empire the world had ever known vanishing – *poof!* – just like that, gone in a puff of smoke, like a magician's party-trick. It was plain that the old ways of doing things were worn out, and that they no longer applied in the modern age.

Road-names were part of it. For centuries, as long as roads had been around, they'd always been called Something Road, and Streets called Something Street, and so on and so forth; but no one, apparently, had ever thought to ask why. This, it was felt, would no longer do. There had been too much unnecessary adornment and frippery for far too long, the thinking went, and it was about time people started behaving rationally.

And so, in 1947, when the planners got down to work on Harlow New Town, roads called roads and streets called streets were to become things of the past. Henceforth, they would just have the functional part of the name, without the redundant descriptor ('Yes, I can see that it's a bloody road – you don't have to tell me that!').

And then there was the Town Centre itself, which was to be truly a Town Centre for the coming age. Because old-style town centres, in the pre-war world, had just happened – they'd grown up higgledy-piggledy over God knows how long, around lanes and alleyways, and were messy and crowded at the best of times; and when there were cars and delivery vans to add to the equation, they really just didn't work any more.

It was now time to go back to the drawing-board and plan the whole thing properly, from scratch.

So Harlow New Town got an urban ring-road, for the traffic to go around, and it got the country's first-ever pedestrian shopping precinct, all planned out by modern planners and designed by modern architects and built – well, probably still built by blokes in flat caps and donkey-jackets with packets of Woodbines in their pockets, but at least they did it using the latest reinforced concrete this time, and put raised walkways all over the place and flat roofs throughout. Which leaked, the roofs – but this was considered a small price to pay for what was manifestly a work of progress. In the words of the great American modernist Frank Lloyd Wright, 'If the roof doesn't leak, the architect hasn't been creative enough.' Or, as he put it, rather more bluntly, to clients who had the temerity to complain about their leaks, 'That's how you can tell it's a roof.'

In 1951 Harlow got the country's first-ever residential tower-block, The Lawn, as a taster of what was to come in the planned communities of the future. And as if all of that weren't enough, to top it off they had sculptures in the parks and squares, so that Art would be for the many, not the few. Not just any sculptures, either – not long-dead generals in classic poses or things like that – but actual Henry Moores. Henry Moores are sort of roundy-shaped things, often with holes in them, and they were considered just the thing at that time – just the business for edifying the population. And the population, no doubt, after being thoroughly edified by the Henry Moores, would all go back up the stairwells of their modern high-rise flats stroking their chins thoughtfully, in order then to listen to a bit of atonal music on their Bakelite wirelesses while getting on with their basket-weaving and smoking their pipes.

It was to be a brave new world of communal solidarity and free dentures and spectacles on the National Health, a world that would see the gradual withering-away of class distinctions, private property, private schools, dirty drains and outdated traditions.

People believed in all that, then. There are still people who believe in it now.

It all depends, I think, on your view of the malleability and perfectibility of human nature: on the one hand, the degree to which we are as we are because, until now, we'd not had enough Progress and hadn't learnt any better; and on the other hand the degree to which we are as we are because that's just the way we are. Back then the balance of opinion among the people who knew best was definitely coming down on the malleability and perfectibility side.

Not just in Harlow, either, but all over the place.

In 1948 – a year after Harlow got going – a professor by the name of B. F. Skinner, the most influential psychologist of his generation, published a book called *Walden Two*, a utopian volume which described the wonderful life lived by the inhabitants of the ultimate 'planned community', a perfect town of a thousand happy, productive and creative people governed by a handful of properly qualified managers and planners, acting on the impartial advice of a small number of scientists. It was a place in which people no longer ate meals at home with their families but dined, instead, in communal canteens, not least because the ratio of volume to surface area of a large cooking-pot is more energy-efficient than that of a smaller one. Clothes no longer denoted status, since status, like poverty and violence, no longer existed – although the people did dress attractively in items carefully and strategically chosen to be beyond the fast-changing vagaries of fashion, which is a bad thing because it 'makes perfectly good clothes worthless' long before they are worn out. And women in this ideal community most certainly did not fill up their wardrobes with party-dresses, since these things were quite clearly impractical. The world, Skinner suggested, could be this way, and people could be this way, with just a little effort from all of us and just a little expert guidance from the likes of him. We could all be this way.

To return to the house, though. I'd had a bit of trouble finding it.

This was because Winchester, or Gatefield, or whatever it was called, wasn't an old-style linear road such as you'd find in an old-style town. It was more of an area, a zone, and it contained a tree-shaped collection of cul-de-sacs, in which all the branches had the same name. So you'd be in it, looking for the house-number, and there'd be other roads branching off to the right and the left, and they'd all have road-signs, and those road-signs would all say exactly the same thing. They were all the same place.

This was modern; confusing, but modern nevertheless.

I found it in the end. In the end, we all found it. There were, I'd say, about twenty of us who turned up there, all crammed into the living-room, sitting four or five to the three-seater sofa, plus one perched on either arm, and three to each armchair, and attempting to drink our tea and eat our Rich Tea biscuits and make conversation with our elbows comprehensively pinned into our sides in the crush, like the arms of Irish dancers.

It was to be a talk arranged by the local organiser of a charity that sent young men and women to far-flung places around the world, to do community work with the local people, and also to have adventures. The leaflet had said that they would be having a famous explorer there to give the talk, although I had not heard of the man before, and neither had the people on either side of me. But we were all up for a bit of adventure in exotic lands, though.

And in he came, tall and upright and dressed in his thick tweed suit and his stout brown shoes, and when he spoke, with his pre-war Etonian drawl, it silenced the room.

'In the past fifty years,' he said, 'we have wiped out the inheritance of the previous 500.'

This was an odd way to start, but then again he had spent the day in Harlow New Town, so perhaps it was to be expected.

'When I was about your age,' he said, looking at us all sitting there before him, looking at the shelves of china and crystal knick-knacks by the faux-mahogany television cabinet, looking at the red plastic Trimphone on the round-edged laminated-teak sideboard, 'when I was about your age, what I wanted, above everything else, was to be an explorer.'

The Emperor's Gift

The top-hatted doorman stood to one side, allowing the young man in the tweed suit to pass through the double revolving doors of the new hotel into the hush of the marble hall, leaving behind all of the sounds of Park Lane, the motor-cars, the taxis, the electric trams, the midday crowds on the pavements.

At the far side of the hall was a great burr-mahogany desk, bound at the corners with beaten copper bands fastened with brass studs, and topped with polished slate, and behind it sat a tall bald man in a tailcoat and gold-braided waistcoat, dipping his pen-nib into a square cut-crystal inkwell as he wrote on the heavy cream-coloured pages of a green leather-covered ledger.

The young man glanced briefly back towards where he had come, and saw the taxi passing back out into the traffic. The square-faced clock between the doors said twenty to three. He was twenty minutes early; but then, everything was riding on this meeting. He crossed the hall, hearing the sound of his own footsteps on the polished floor.

The man at the desk looked up.

'Mr Thesiger?' he said. 'You are expected. One moment.'

He picked up a small bell and shook it.

Instantly, a second man appeared by his side, as if from nowhere.

'If you would be so kind as to follow me, sir,' said the man.

He led the young man through the hotel, past the open doors through which could be seen the vast pillarless ballroom, and to a secluded table in the restaurant beyond, where two places had been laid and where two waiters stood, each with a starched napkin over his forearm.

They brought the young man tea, and a silver tiered stand of cucumber sandwiches and small pastries.

He took some tea, but did not touch the food. He took the fob-watch from his waistcoat pocket, and turned it over in his fingers, and then put it back again. The walls and coffered ceilings were white and gold, as were the fish-scale-patterned Egyptian pillars. The pale carpet was intricately woven in a chinoiserie style.

He consulted his watch again. Still almost twenty minutes left to wait.

He had, by now, made the decision to go.

He would, he had decided, cross the desert to Aussa, and he would enter the Sultan's kingdom and pass through, and he would follow the river along all the length of its unmarked, unknown course until he came to the end and solved the mystery. On this he was determined.

He had made arrangements and plans, and had obtained the blessing and sponsorship of the Royal Geographical Society, and gained further funds for food and equipment, medicines and wages for his party from Magdalen College and from the Linnean Society.

But at this time the Sultanate of Aussa lay, nominally, within the borders of Abyssinia, and obtaining the permission of the Abyssinian Government was proving considerably more difficult than he had bargained for.

His initial requests had been met with a flat refusal; and although he was not without connections there, although his late father had been British Minister at the court of the former Emperor

Menelik, although he himself had received a personal invitation to attend the coronation of Haile Selassie, these things seemed to have got him nowhere.

And then came the message from the Embassy.

The waiter came, to see if fresh tea was required. It was not.

The young man felt his watch-chain again, and half-pulled his watch from its pocket, but then pushed it back, and instead studied the scalloped pattern on the back of his teaspoon.

Time. How we measure it out. How it feels, the passing of it. How what was is transformed utterly into what is, and which even in the moment of perceiving has vanished into what is to come, and so on for ever and always. How the wood that made the table at which he sat had grown, for however many years, in some far-flung forest, and the ragged trailing creepers overhanging, and the piercing call of brightly plumed birds. This same thing.

His father. The presence of him, the fact of him, as solid and real as anything in this life, and now gone, long, long gone: dead and buried these what – thirteen years? One wonders how this can be so.

He became aware of low voices across the room, and of a cluster of men, and one stepped out from among them and gestured to the others to stay, and turned to look over to where Thesiger sat. He was a young man – little more than a boy, in fact – maybe sixteen or seventeen at a guess – and slight, light-boned, narrow-shouldered and black as your hat. He had prominent ears, big, heavy-lidded eyes, and he wore a formal black suit, tightly buttoned-up, with a high white collar, and highly-polished black shoes on his feet; and he carried a battered leather satchel, brass-buckled like a doctor's bag.

Thesiger shot to his feet, recognising the boy at once.

The boy smiled, revealing white teeth, and crossed to where he stood.

'Do sit down,' he said, in perfect, educated English, 'You don't mind if I join you?'

'You are more than welcome, sir,' said Thesiger.

A waiter appeared and pulled out a chair so that His Highness Asfa Wossen Tafari, Crown Prince of Abyssinia, eldest son of the Conquering Lion of the Tribe of Judah, King of Kings and Elect of God, and direct lineal descendant, it was said, of King Solomon and the Queen of Sheba, could sit down.

'Jolly good sandwiches,' said the boy, taking a bite, 'Not so sure about the tea, though. A bit cool for my liking.'

He snapped his fingers and fresh tea was brought.

'Now,' he said, 'down to business. The place you desire to go to: they are very bad people there, you know. Absolute savages. And you are determined to go among them?'

'Yes, sir.'

'They will kill you, of course.'

'I'm prepared to take my chances.'

'I am sure that you are. Everything I have heard about you convinces me that this is, indeed, the case. But it is not as simple as that. Not by a long way, because if they kill you, it puts my father in a very difficult position.'

'How so, sir?'

'Aussa is part of Abyssinia. This is agreed. It is not in dispute. And in all of Abyssinia my father's word is law. But the Sultan does not always see things in this way. And there have been . . . incidents in the past. Very unfortunate ones. We tend to keep our officials away from Aussa, to avoid too many of these . . . misunderstandings. Now, if you travel there, with my father's authority and under his protection, and if anything were to happen to you, then he would be obliged to take the matter up with the Sultan, and it would all be rather awkward.'

'I understand that, sir – which is why I am prepared to go there at my own risk, and without involving your father in any way, other than asking for his permission to proceed.'

'Hmm . . .' he said. 'Just what we expected you to say. So you are absolutely determined to do this thing?'

'I am, sir.'

'And nothing we could say would make you think otherwise?'

'No. Nothing.'

The young prince looked serious for a while, and then, quite suddenly, he smiled.

'Well, in that case, my father has, after careful consideration, authorised me to offer you two things.'

He took a sip of his tea, savouring the flavour of it before continuing.

'The first,' he said, 'is his permission.'

Thesiger moved as if to speak, but the prince raised a hand to silence him. 'And the second,' he continued, 'is this.'

He pulled out his satchel from beneath the table and unfastened the buckles. From inside a faint, slightly sour odour arose, as of stale sweat.

Reaching in, the prince pulled out a bundle of yellowed cloth, which looked very much like someone's used shirt, rolled up and knotted around something weighty; he passed it across the table.

'You may open it.'

It was, indeed, an old shirt. But when Thesiger untied the knotted sleeves and unwrapped the bundle, he saw inside a heavy, ancient-looking gold chain upon which were strung rows of thick gold rings.

'For your expenses,' said the prince.

Don't Tell Others

Sometimes there can be whole days, weeks, months and years that pass you by and it seems just like the blink of an eye.

Then there are other times where the actions of an instant seem to last for ever.

People who have been in car crashes or other near-fatal disasters often talk about time 'slowing down'. It is said that they are able to recall all sorts of peripheral detail with astonishing accuracy, as if they had the time, in the half-second of their almost-death, to roam the scene with the camera of their mind's eye, and to record for posterity not just the look of drunken horror on the other driver's face but the missing second button on his shirt-front; the colour and style of the lead on the dog being walked by the man in the flat cap on the pavement; the words and the patterns on the half-torn circus poster on the wall behind him.

Scientists call this *time dilation*, and it signifies the feeling of the opening-out of a moment far beyond its normal or expected limits.

There is a reason that it feels like this.

At moments of intense significance and at moments of great physical risk, the brain pulls in all of its resources and processing-power, and crams more observations and more reactions into a fraction of a second than it would normally make use of in a duration many, many times longer. It does this the better to react quickly and effectively, and so to cope with whatever challenges or opportunities it faces.

The result of all of this is that we experience moments that, for good or ill, are more intensely lived, and in which time appears to slow down, or even, on occasion, to stop.

And just as this time dilation exists, so also, I believe, there exists its opposite, which you might, I suppose, call *time diminution*, if you were to use the same rules of construction. Time diminution, or what you will, is an experience in which large tracts and expanses of time just pass you by, just vanish away unmarked and unnoticed, except when you look back later and think, was that it?, or, where did it all go?

From the end of the talk in the house in the cul-de-sac in Harlow New Town to my next contact with the man, and the visit to his flat in Tite Street, was two years, more or less.

They were two years in which, in one sense, much happened, but in which, in another, the main thing that happened was the passing away of time.

When the meeting had ended, the people there gathered up their coats, and those who drove got out their car-keys, while for those who did not, minicabs and the cars of parents arrived outside. But when he had finished his talk, and when the evening had begun to break up, I went up to him and asked him more questions about his life and times, and we carried on talking even as others were leaving around us, until, at last, there were no other guests left, and the owner of the house was standing there, as if to say, well, haven't you got a home to go to? The man took a scrap of paper from his pocket and wrote his address on it and handed it to me.

'If you go on this trip,' he said, 'do write and let me know how you get on.'

And then it was outside into the night air.

I applied, but did not get a place.

I also applied for academic scholarships overseas, but did not get them, either.

In the meantime, there was banking to be done, and banking examinations, which I was required to study for.

Months passed in which I undertook two correspondence courses with something called the Rapid Results College. One was in Law Relating to Banking and the other in Economics. In Economics I learnt – the only thing I remember from it now – that if a bank lends money that doesn't exist, and which hasn't been minted or printed, or made or planned, it can actually cause that money to come into being, and so increase the money supply.

This is something of a paradox, on a number of levels, in the way that Heisenberg's Uncertainty Principle is in physics. One of the main levels upon which it is a paradox is that it is, according to the experts, clearly and demonstrably true; and yet, at the exact same time, it has the ability to seem to me to be the most complete and utter nonsense.

At some point during that time I reapplied for the overseas scheme and this time was offered a place. It was to be a trip to America, involving trail-building in the Rocky Mountains and the Appalachians, and also drilling wells for water on a Sioux Indian reservation on the edge of the Badlands in South Dakota.

I still had the scrap of paper Wilfred Thesiger had given me.

I wrote and told him about it.

About a week later a cream-coloured envelope arrived on my doormat.

Inside was a cheque for £300, drawn on a London private bank; and with the cheque was a three-word letter, written in blue-black fountain-pen on embossed headed notepaper.

It said, 'Don't tell others.'

The Clinic

The doctor had my notes on the desk in front of him, in a buff card file.

'You understand,' he said, removing the stethoscope from around his neck and placing it on the desk beside the file, 'that before I can give you the result of your test I am required to offer you counselling. This is our standard procedure. It doesn't presuppose a positive result, or indeed a negative one.'

The clinic was in Charlotte Street, in the West End of London.

I had come to be there as the result of a conversation with a friend, who, as a student, had spent a year doing voluntary work for a telephone advice line.

'You did *what*?' he'd said, aghast, 'With *who*? You want to get yourself checked out, mate. You could have anything, you know, absolutely anything.'

And then, over the next hour or so, he'd told me in great detail about the counselling work he'd done, and how, in particular, I should watch out for any swelling or discomfort in my armpits.

'It always starts there, you know.'

And, indeed, now that he mentioned it, it did feel somewhat uncomfortable there. I'd put it down to it being a warm day and my wearing a slightly tight shirt with rough seams. But the more I thought about it, the more noticeable the feeling became.

'Now,' said the doctor, 'a few questions for you. Are you an intravenous drug user?'

'Do I look like one?'

'You'd be surprised.'

'I've never even been drunk.'

'Fine. I'll take that as a "no", then. And have you ever had a blood transfusion?'

'No.'

'So tell me, in your own words, why you think you might have placed yourself at risk of contracting this virus.'

'I was on an Indian reservation.'

'Go on . . .'

'In America, and they had this thing called the Sun Dance, and I got invited to it by the man whose land we were working on, and he said it was something of an honour, because they didn't normally let white people go along.'

'So. You went to a dance. With a man. And then . . .?'

'Well, they hold it in a circle, the Sun Dance, and they have a big sort of maypole thing in the centre, with cords coming down from it. The dance goes on for three days, and when we arrived it was at the beginning of the third day, and the dancers looked not quite there, if you know what I mean. Stripped to the waist, and sort of swaying backwards and forwards, and their eyes not quite focused – or focused beyond what they were looking at. And there was this constant drumming, three men sitting side by side, beating these big drums for all they were worth, and singing these strange guttural songs, and then the dancers all smoked a pipe that had burning sage in it, and they went off into a sort of tent thing, which was a sweat-lodge, like a sauna, with hot coals inside – and it was well over a hundred degrees outside, too, so you could only imagine the heat inside.'

'Did you go into the sauna with these men?'

'No. I wasn't allowed to. It was for the dancers only.'

'But you would have liked to?'

'Yes, I suppose I would. To know what it was like in there. But it wasn't really an option. Anyway, they came back out after a while and they arranged themselves around the edge of the circle, and the drums and the singing got louder and they began swaying forwards and backwards; and then one of the dancers crossed over into the circle and lay down on his back at the feet of an older man, who was the medicine man. The medicine man had a knife in his hand and he bent down and made four cuts in the dancer's chest, two above each nipple, and then he took two skewers made of eagle-bone from a pouch at his waist and pushed them through the holes he had made, and attached them to two cords coming down from the pole. The dancer got up and began to dance backwards until the cords pulled tight. And then another dancer lay down, and another and another until they were all strung up to the pole. And you could see that some of them had done it quite a few times before, because of the rows of scars on their chests. And then they danced backwards and forwards, backwards and forwards to the music. And meanwhile an old man went into the circle and knelt down, and the medicine man made cuts in his back and attached cords to them to which he tied a buffalo skull; and then a small child climbed onto the skull and the old man stood up and began to drag the skull, with the child still on it, around the outside of the circle.

'And the music got louder and louder and the dancers danced more intensely, pulling back harder against the cords with each pass, until at length one danced right up almost to the foot of the pole and then ran backwards, arms outspread, pulling with all his weight and snapping the skewers in his chest. Then it was the turn of the next dancer.

'Meanwhile, I became aware of a queue forming over to one side of the circle, a line of people, young and old, male and female, all baring their shoulders. Up at the head of the queue stood a medicine man and his assistant, and as each person approached, they did something to each arm in turn, and the person came away with blood running down them.

'I asked my companion what was happening and he said that the people in the queue were friends and relatives of the dancers, and they were each giving what he described as an "offering".

'And it struck me then that it would be only polite, only good manners, for me to do the same.

'When I got to the front of the queue the medicine man's assistant took hold of my arm with one hand, and with the other he pushed a pin or needle into my skin and lifted it up towards the medicine man, who took a small, sharp knife and ran it smartly up the needle, nicking the top of the skin, and causing the blood to flow. Then they did the same on the other arm. And then, using the same knife and the same pin, they did the same to the next person, and the next and the next.

'And that,' I said, 'was why I came to have a blood test.'

There was a slight pause, during which the doctor appeared to shake himself slightly, as if waking from some private reverie.

I was aware that I had been talking for quite some time.

'Well,' he said, 'let's say between ourselves that this *was* your reason for coming here. But really, in this day and age, you know, it is *perfectly* acceptable to have issues with your . . . *personal orientation*. Absolutely fine. Just so long as you take the appropriate precautions. You'll find details in the leaflets you'll get on your way out. Oh, and your test result is negative. Congratulations.'

Preparations

Two weeks later I was at Thesiger's flat, with the books and the sword, the paintings and the photographs, drinking too much sherry than was good for me and talking about travel. I didn't mention the clinic experience, though. It didn't seem the place to do so.

And he invited me out to Africa, and said he would show me the country round about, and I asked – I don't think I mentioned this earlier – but I asked if he minded at all if I brought two companions along; my brother Frazer and my friend Andy. He replied, 'Well, if they're anything like you, it will be a pleasure to see them.'

'They are,' I said.

Although on what level Andy – black athlete with a Mohican haircut – may be thought to be 'like me' is, perhaps, a matter for debate; but he was a good travelling companion. He'd been with me in America, building trails in the mountains, and was blessed with an extraordinarily even temperament and an ability to take more or less anything in his stride. Like the clear, sunny day, for example, on top of a bare rocky ridge high above the treeline, when we were caught, quite suddenly, by a violent electrical storm that appeared out of nowhere, as they do in those parts. There was no shelter and nowhere to hide, and a steep drop on either side, and the lightning began to hit the ground around us, so close that we could smell the singed granite boulders just feet away from where we stood.

I was overwhelmed by fear and panic, and the sheer size and force of the storm, the power of it; and I screamed at Andy to take his pack off and get down on the ground. He considered my words carefully, rain hammering down on his head and lightning striking all around him, then removed first one arm and then the other from his rucksack, upon which hung a large aluminium cooking-pot. This done, he put it neatly down on the ground and crouched down beside it. He was like that.

He was keen on the idea of going to Africa when I told him about it.

'Is it going to be tough going, do you think?'

'Maybe,' I said, 'but then again he is eighty, this Thesiger, so there's probably a limit to how tough.'

I booked our flights with Aeroflot, on account of it being the very cheapest airline I could find, by about £5; and in the mistaken assumption that one airline is very much like any other.

The Awash Station

The Awash Station was not an inspiring place to be at the best of times.

It was a low whitewashed bungalow, tin-roofed, built by the French and plonked down in the middle of nowhere on a wide, dusty plain, by the side of railway tracks that stretch off endlessly into the distance in either direction, linking Addis Ababa with what was then French Somaliland, and which is now called Djibouti.

Behind the station stood the optimistically named Buffet de la Gare, where lodging, of a kind, and food, of a kind, could be obtained by travellers who had no other choice.

For the fifteen Abyssinian soldiers who had been chosen by their superiors, on Government orders, to await the arrival of the Englishman, it was even less than inspiring.

It was to be these men's duty to accompany him on his expedition to Aussa, to provide protection for his convoy – in much the same way, in fact, that the far larger party of Egyptian soldiers, with their two cannons, had provided protection for the Swiss Munzinger's convoy in 1875 – until, that is, they were all horribly murdered.

For the Danakil, it mattered little what a stranger did for his living, whether soldier, explorer or whatever: what mattered was the kill, and the all-important trophies to be obtained from them to increase a man's status and his standing among his companions.

An earlier English traveller on the borders of their land recounted in his diary how one of his servants, accompanied by a Danakil guide, had gone down to the river to bathe. No sooner had this servant put down his rifle and stepped into the water than the guide picked the gun up, shot him dead, cut off his genitals with his dagger and went off back home with the trophy to celebrate his achievement. And his fellow-tribesmen had, no doubt, slapped him heartily on the back as he recounted his story, and roared with mirth at the details, exclaiming, 'What larks!' or its Danakil equivalent, and accounted him a mighty fine fellow for what he had done.

So when the Englishman did turn up, eventually, at the Awash Station, the soldiers made no secret of their lack of enthusiasm for him and his scheme; and they were altogether less than diligent, and altogether less than enthusiastic, in helping load up the camels and doing whatever else it was that he expected them to do.

Nor was the mood lightened in any way by the recent announcement by the inhabitants of Bahdu, one of the biggest Asaimara territories along the course of the Awash River, that they had renounced any semblance of allegiance to the Government, and that furthermore they would refuse to pay any tribute demanded of them. And if the Emperor didn't like it, he could stick it in his pipe and smoke it. Or words to that effect.

Thesiger, meanwhile, was more concerned about the fact that in the circumstances someone in authority might take it into his head to cancel his expedition; and, sure enough, he soon received a telephone message from an official saying that there was now fierce fighting in the province, and that the expedition would need at least a hundred armed men to stand more than one chance in ten of survival; which, of course, was quite out of the question. In the circumstances, therefore, his fifteen soldiers would be recalled forthwith, and he would be best advised to go back to wherever it was he came from and forget all about it. To which Thesiger responded by pulling rank – reminding the official that the Emperor himself had authorised the journey – and then by bribing the Awash Station telephone operator to stay away from his office, so that no further communications would be able to get through.

And so it was, on this happy and optimistic note, that the party loaded up their camels and set off into the wilderness.

Aeroflot

As a child, I once watched a sketch on a television comedy show –
The Benny Hill Show, it was – about a man who wants to go on
holiday. He goes to the travel-agent, and when he gets there he is
offered the choice of two rival operators. I can't remember the
names of the companies now, but let's say that they were called
Bennytours and Cheapdeals, for the sake of argument. They both
seemed to offer more or less the same thing – same destination,
same flight, same hotel and so on and so forth, but with the
difference that Cheapdeals (or whatever they were called) was
ever-so-slightly cheaper. It was an infinitesimal difference; absolutely tiny – let's say that the Bennytours holiday cost £40 and the
Cheapdeals holiday cost £39 19s 6d, or thereabouts. It was a long
time ago.

So our man bought the Cheapdeals ticket, as you would.

And then there followed one single joke, which was dragged
out for about half an hour. The joke was this: the Cheapdeals
holidaymakers were herded onto the plane with electric cattleprods
by boot-faced Russian shotputter-types and served cold gruel and
whatever as their in-flight meal, while the Bennytours people, up
at the front of the same plane but tantalisingly visible beyond a
flimsy curtain, got velvet chaises longues and champagne, and

grapes individually peeled by beautiful air hostesses in barely covered underwear. And then you got endless variations on the same joke over and over again in the hotel, at the pool, at dinner, on the way home. At the age of eight I found it all hilarious.

But when I saw it on the television, back then, what I thought was that it was comedy, and I thought that it was something that someone, probably Benny Hill himself, had made up.

It wasn't until I chose an Aeroflot flight to Nairobi in preference to one with Saudi Air – for the sake of saving £5 – that I realised it was actually a closely observed documentary. Except that with Aeroflot the experience lasted for eighteen hours each way, and the joke, if ever there was one, wore thin considerably sooner.

It was not so much the length of the flight, although it was, all in all, more than twice as long as you might have expected, given the distance. This was down to all the stops – stops which included several hours in Larnaka airport; followed by eight very long hours sitting on the floor in Moscow airport, there not being enough chairs there for all who wanted them; followed then by several hours in the sweltering airport in Aden, in the People's Democratic Republic of Yemen, which at that time had rows of bullet-holes in the windows from the recent coup attempt.

Nor was it the extreme poverty and paucity of the food and drink we were served – that's what you expect when you pay as little as you possibly can for your flight. And we were, in fact, given complimentary refreshments in Yemen. The refreshments consisted of half a plastic cup of flat-looking cherryade. Which would have been delicious, I am sure, had I not put mine down on the bar for a moment, upon which the barman took it away and gave it to someone else. I did ask for another, but the barman, being unable to speak English, called in the assistance of a man in sunglasses carrying a sub-machine gun. This man couldn't speak

English, either, but by gesticulating at me with his gun he was better able to communicate to me the fact that I should have drunk my drink when I was given it, and that I should now stop being a nuisance and forget all about it, if I knew what was good for me.

But to be fair to Aeroflot, they had at least arranged for their passengers to have in-flight entertainment. This entertainment came in the form of a battered magazine – one copy per row of seats – in which could be found all manner of tempting advertisements for combine harvesters and industrial machinery – should we feel the urge to splash out and treat ourselves to one, just for the hell of it. It also contained a full-page picture of a rather beefy young lady in a bikini standing by the edge of a particularly icy-looking sea, beneath a slate-grey sky, with the words 'Come to Sunny Crimea' printed above her head. This alone was enough, almost, to make the even most hardened Western imperialist-capitalist lackey want to defect instantly to the Soviet Workers' Paradise. Which, I am sure, was the intention.

It was none of these things that made the flight so unpleasant.

Instead, it was the sheer grim, unrelenting joylessness with which every aspect of the entire journey was conducted, from beginning to end.

If any of the stewardesses smiled, even momentarily, at any point throughout the entire eighteen hours, then I did not see it.

Raiders of the Dressing-up Box

When we walked out, the three of us, into the sunlight of Nairobi's crowded streets, dressed in our outfits, one could only begin to imagine how impressed the locals were at the sight of us.

I had gone for the 'Old-Style Boy Scout Meets British Explorer' look: khaki shirt with epaulettes and pleated breast-pockets, slightly-too-large khaki shorts, broad belt with a knife at my waist – the sort of thing, in fact, that Thesiger might himself have worn some half a century before; the sort of thing that his uncle, Lord Chelmsford, would have seen his men wearing, further ago still, if he'd paid an unexpected visit to a British Army hill station somewhere near Poona during his years as Viceroy of India. Although I did, also, have a black-and-white Arab headscarf worn around my neck as a sort of cravat, and also as a sort of sartorial homage to Lawrence of Arabia.

My brother had taken a similar approach.

Andy, meanwhile, had gone for more of an Indiana Jones effect, topped off with a broad-brimmed olive-green felt hat.

It lasted for about five minutes, the hat, until a small boy darted out from among the crowds, snatched the thing off his head and shot off again, weaving in and out of the passers-by like a greased piglet.

Runner that he was, Andy set off after the boy, though he was encumbered by a large and bulky rucksack.

We caught up with Andy about ten minutes later, standing by the side of the road catching his breath.

'Did you see that?' he said. 'The little . . .'

He sought for the most appropriate word, but before it could come to him he broke into a grin.

'Well,' he said, 'whatever. He could run, though, couldn't he?'

No hat. And no Mohican hairstyle any more, either; he'd shaved it off for the trip. I'd asked him to.

'Andy,' I'd said, 'he's a very proper sort of man. He wouldn't appreciate it, you know; not unless it was part of your traditional costume or something.'

Which, in the wilds of south London, it is not.

'O wad some pow'r the giftie gie' us,' as Robert Burns said, 'to see oursels as others see us.'

And I'm sure we would all three of us have been suitably impressed, had it been.

The Danakil, murderous and treacherous though they were, nevertheless set great store by their appearance, and had an elaborate code of traditional bodily adornments and modifications. A curved dagger worn across the stomach, bearing a row of brass-bound thongs; an ostrich-feather plume, worn Red Indian-style; slit earlobes; a coloured loincloth; these were all signifiers, in their world. What they signified – them being Danakil and all –was death, and each decoration recorded the number and kind of victims killed, and the manner of death given them.

But as for the Danakil and his death-tokens, so too for the City banker and his pinstripes; for the High Court judge and his wig and gown; for the medicine man and his feathered bonnet and the witchdoctor and his carved mask. And also the graduate and is mortar-board; the bride and her wedding-dress and the Queen and her crown and robes of state. The costume is the outward form and signifier of how we see ourselves and of how we want others to see us. Or rather it's more than that, or it's other than that; and the act of wearing it makes you somehow more than you are, and other than you are; and for a while you become the living form of something bigger than you are, and more than you are, and which existed long before you were born and which will go on long after you are dust. Or something.

There was a British Prime Minister, Gordon Brown, who in his years as Chancellor of the Exchequer, would turn up at the Lord Mayor's Banquet wearing what was variously described by his aides as 'working dress' and as 'a business suit'. All the other guests, meanwhile, arrived in formal white tie and tails, as the dress-code required. In doing this, Brown succeeded in wearing the most ostentatious costume in the room, a costume which said – depending on your point of view – 'progressive, modern reformer', or 'dour, miserable killjoy puritan', or else, in the words of the journalist Simon Heffer, 'simply bloody rude'.

In the town where I now live, my wife and I once saw a party of schoolgirls looking very smart and striking, all dressed in long scarlet cloaks and wearing broad straw hats. A few years later, we took our eldest daughter, Alice – ten years old at the time – to the school to be interviewed by the headmistress, who had taken up her post at more or less the same time that we had first seen the girls. As we entered her office, Alice was wearing the winter uniform of her own primary school, a dark blue pinafore with a woollen coat and a felt hat.

'My word!' exclaimed the headmistress. 'How very quaint!'

She crouched down to speak to Alice on her level.

'Well,' she said, 'you won't have to worry about that sort of thing here, you know: we got rid of our hats years ago!'

And at about the same time, a man by the name of Mr Philip Collins, the director of something called the Social Market Foundation, published a pamphlet calling for an end to costumes and all other 'outdated flummery' in public life:

'It is time we had an honours system that does not satirise itself . . . the whole bizarre panoply of OBEs, MBEs, CBEs, DCVOs, MVOs, GCBs, CHs, MNOGs and Yeomen Bed Goers should be put on the bonfire along with the vanity of those who care for such distinctions. We should abolish the titles of Sir and Dame into the bargain. Instead of all this nonsense we should establish a single award, the Order of Merit . . . awarded at a new democratic ceremony, performed at the House of Commons by the Speaker, *dressed in clothes he would be happy to wear on public transport.*'

So, a bus driver's uniform, then.

And perhaps the honours themselves might be dispensed from a form of ticket-machine which the Speaker wears on a strap about his neck.

On which note, we met up with our bus at the allotted place, in a bus garage in the middle of a shanty-town on the edge of the city, where we were welcomed on board by a bus driver who, though he lacked an official uniform, did have a ticket-machine – an old aluminium London bus conductor's one, slung across his shoulder on a strap made of knotted string – and who was a model driver in almost every other way. Smiling broadly, he loaded our rucksacks into the baggage hold and showed us to our seats, while helping old ladies to stow baskets of live chickens in the overhead racks and collecting money and handing out tickets, laughing and bantering all the while. He was, as I say – uniform aside – the perfect driver in almost every respect. The only respect, in fact, in which he fell in any way short, was in his total inability to actually drive a bus. As we were soon to discover.

You Can Run But You Can't Hide

The telephone call to the provincial governor's office was in Amharic. Probably.

Either way, there exists no transcript of it.

But if you had been there, if you had been listening in – in the next office, say – and if you'd understood the language, then I imagine that what you would have heard would have sounded something like this:

'He said *what*, you say?'

'Oh, did he, now? He's having a laugh, isn't he? And then what?'

'Nothing? What d'you mean, *nothing*?'

'Not answering the telephone? How can they not be answering the telephone? They've got a telephone operator. That's what he does. He operates the bloody telephone. That's what he's paid to do.'

'Oh, really? Has he, now? Well, we need to have words with that operator. Strong words. And this Englishman, he's done *what*, now? Gone? Gone where? I don't believe it!'

'Yes, well you make sure that you bloody well do.'

The sound of a phone being slammed back down in its cradle.

'Right, young fellow-me-lad – I'm going to put a stop to your little game. You see if I don't!'

And meanwhile, out in the wild lands, the little party was making its way slowly onwards across a semi-desert plain of dust and scrub. They walked well into the night, there being a full moon, and Thesiger anxious to put as much distance as he could between himself and the provincial authorities. All in all there were thirty-nine of them: Thesiger himself, the fifteen conscripted soldiers, twenty-two Somali bearers and camel-men and one Danakil from the Awash Station, who was there in the dual role of guide and hostage, and whose main duty, apart from showing the way, was to call out into the wilderness in his language at regular intervals throughout the day and night, saying that they were armed to the teeth, and that whoever came near would be shot.

That night, however, the guide – or hostage – tried to bolt, but was caught. After that, he was escorted everywhere he went by two armed guards.

The next morning they set off early, and soon entered the territory of the Adoimara band of the Danakil tribe, where they came across a village, in which a great feast was taking place.

They sent an armed party down to the village to make contact, and to see what was happening. It was, they discovered, a funeral feast for a party of men ambushed and killed by their Asaimara rivals at a spot not 200 yards from where the expedition had camped the previous night.

The villagers were expecting a further raid by the Asaimara at any time. This was fortunate for Thesiger, because it meant that he and his armed party were welcomed as potential allies.

They were invited to share in the feast, and were also taken out to see the bloodstained rocks where the attack had taken place. They also learnt that it was here that the party of Greeks had been killed by Asaimara warriors some years previously; and that an Adoimara headman called Omar from their village had found the sole survivor and taken him to safety, in order to obtain a reward from the Government.

This Omar, they said, was a man well known for his skills in dealing with outsiders, whether they be Government officials or rival tribesmen, or even half-dead Greeks. Which suggested a way of easing the progress of the expedition.

After much negotiation, and after the payment of large numbers of goods and animals to both Omar himself and to more or less his entire extended family, it was agreed that the headman would be their guide on the next stage of the journey – which would take them through the foothills of Mount Ayelu and into Bahdu on the other side, through which the river flowed on its way to Aussa, and where the Asaimara lived in great numbers.

So it was that they set off the next morning, walking throughout the day as the ground became steadily higher and more rugged as they approached Mount Ayelu, and at length they found themselves at the entrance to a narrow pass in the hills, beyond which lay Bahdu. At this point Omar called for the party to halt, and urged them all, before they pressed on, to beware, to keep their wits about them, and above all to stay close together and not to straggle, as the less-than-willing soldiers had a tendency to do, for they were now at a place, he said, where ambushes were known to happen.

This they did, and they made their way through the pass without incident, although from time to time men saw – or thought they saw – movements in the rocks above; but when they pointed the sites of these movements out to others, there was always nothing to be seen.

Upon reaching the other side they found themselves on the edge of a broad, surprisingly fertile plain, dotted with trees and mat-covered huts and about a mile wide, through which the Awash wound its way slowly on. And as they moved across this plain they saw some distance ahead of them, by the water's edge, squatting in groups beneath the shade of those trees, sharpening their daggers and their spear-tips, tamping down the powder in their antique muskets, a great host of Asaimara warriors, already some 200 strong; and many more hurrying to join them from every side.

An Interrupted Journey

Outside, the bus smelt of diesel. Inside, it also smelt of diesel, but more so.

It was deemed to be full when it became physically impossible to cram into it any more people, chickens, bags and boxes than filled the seats, aisles and overhead luggage-racks, even by pushing; and so the driver climbed into his seat, inserted and turned his key, and with a great shudder and a cloud of black smoke, the engine burst into life. Then it promptly shut down again. A second attempt brought nothing but a dry whirring. On the third go the thing got up and running; and so, with an audible crunch, the driver jammed the engine into gear and the bus jerked suddenly forward, sending bystanders scattering and bags tumbling from the racks onto the heads of passengers.

It headed out of the garage and – without first stopping to see if anything was coming – lurched out into the street. Thankfully, many of the oncoming vehicles had brakes in various degrees of working order, and so it was that the bus managed to take the corner and make its way into the flow of traffic, and without any deaths or serious injuries, as far as I could see.

The driver turned around and gave a great beaming smile at his passengers – for a worrying length of time, in my estimation, given that we were moving at a fair lick by now; and then he turned his face back to the front and slammed his foot down on the accelerator, pinning us into the backs of our seats, just in time to cross a traffic-light which had recently turned an attractive shade of red; and just in time to give a cheery wave to the driver of the car that had been crossing the junction at the time, and which, by some miracle, managed to swerve out of the way.

And on we went; and at some point in the journey, the driver seemed to have noticed – perhaps for the first time – that the bus was fitted with a sort of stick thing just below the steering-wheel, and that by moving it about into different positions it was possible to cause the engine to make all manner of entertaining noises, from high-pitched metallic shrieks to low, shuddering growls; and that, moreover, these sounds were all accompanied by actions of various kinds, including judders and lurches, near-stops and starts, and sudden, mad accelerations just as someone was about to cross the road in front of him. And given that it was going to be rather a long journey, he took the opportunity to make full use of all of these possibilities, more or less constantly, all the way through the city and out into the land beyond.

The passengers, meanwhile, or most of them, seemed to see what was happening as perfectly normal, as par for the course, as golfers say, and as part and parcel of taking a bus; and they sat back and chatted to each other, or looked out of the windows smiling to themselves, even as chickens and metal cooking-pots fell about their heads.

The journey was scheduled to take some eight hours to cover the hundred miles north to Thompson's Falls, where we were to meet a second bus; but after we had been driving for about an hour we became aware of a strange metallic wailing noise from beneath the floor, and the bus began to shudder and slow down, and the driver pulled over to the side of the road, climbed down from his seat and opened a large hatch in the aisle between the seats, revealing the grease-encrusted engine, within which was a tube from which a brown liquid spurted directly upwards, as from a punctured artery.

Having satisfied himself that he had discovered the source of the problem, the driver closed the hatch on it, started the engine up again and drove on. We managed to get almost another hour out of the bus before the noise and the shuddering became markedly worse, and we made a second roadside stop.

This time, it was apparent that something was seriously amiss; but the driver was onto it. Rummaging around in his glove-compartment, he pulled out a plastic bag, which he wrapped around the tube. This made an immediate difference. No sooner had he done it than the brown liquid instantly stopped spurting upwards. Instead, it spurted sideways. Or at least, it spurted sideways for a few moments until the bag melted, and then it started to spurt upwards again. But at least something had been done, and that was the important thing, and so we were ready – once the hatch was closed – to set off again.

We drove on, climbing painfully slowly as the land around us rose, the engine shrieking fit to burst, and as we did so we left behind the dust and dirt of the city and its surrounding plains and entered lush farmland where coffee and tea grew. At length, though, we spluttered to a halt, by an iron water-tank on the edge of a village called Nyeri, a place of tin-roofed breeze-block huts. From a church in the village, some fifty yards from where we sat, came the sounds of drumming and singing.

The driver got out and came back with a man with a spanner, who removed the tube and took it away.

There we remained for two hours, while a steadily growing crowd of small children gathered around to watch.

Eventually the man came back with the driver, and together they tinkered with the engine until both seemed satisfied, and then they closed the hatch and loaded us all on board, and after three or four false starts got the engine going again, the cloud of smoke sending the children running; and we set off once more on the road to the north.

As we drove on, the land became flatter and drier, with breeze-block and mud-hut villages surrounded by banana trees and fields of tea and coffee bushes becoming fewer and farther between and giving way, at last, to broad savannah. And once we were truly out, at last, way, way out in the middle of nowhere and away from all settlement, then the bus took its one big chance to do the thing for which it had been rehearsing the whole journey long: it stopped, dead, and packed up for good, and no amount of opening and closing of hatches or wrapping and unwrapping of plastic bags could do anything to coax even the faintest flicker of life from it. That was it, finished.

All there was left for us to do was to get off, pick up our bags and walk.

The driver stood in the doorway of his bus as we all set off with our rucksacks and our parcels and our pots and our chickens, and waved us off with one last cheery smile.

The River-Plain of Bahdu

The small party carried on across the plain; and when it drew near to where the warriors had gathered it halted, and two men – Thesiger and Omar the Adoimara headman – stepped out alone and approached them, calling out greetings and salutations. Which were not returned; or rather, which were returned with a sullen and belligerent silence, by spitting upon the ground, by the drawing of knives and the cocking of muskets, and each man pointedly turning his back on the two outsiders as they approached, in deliberate insult.

Sensing that things were likely to get worse rather than better, Thesiger and Omar returned to the men and instructed them to unpack the camels and to make camp, in the open and with a clear field of fire all around, taking care to build a perimeter wall around it using packs and equipment. As they did so, warriors began to gather around to watch, and upon hearing the camel-men talk, some began to poke them and prod them, and to accuse them of belonging to the Issa, a Somali-speaking tribe with whom they were perpetually at war. As, indeed, they were perpetually at war with most other tribes in the vicinity, and with many more besides.

Upon which it struck Thesiger as a good idea to take down his empty rifle-case and to refer to it, loudly and pointedly, as 'the machine gun'. This was something that others among his party quickly picked up on, in their various languages.

It appeared to have some effect, at least in the short term, in that it caused a number of the warriors to draw back a little way, muttering among themselves and pointing, and muttering again, and generally giving serious consideration to the possibility of all being mown down.

Some, however, were overheard saying that if they did not kill the entire party now, then they would most certainly come back and do so after nightfall.

The headman Omar, meanwhile, sensing the way things were going, set off through the hostile crowd, frantically trying to find someone in authority with whom he could negotiate.

He first found an Asaimara headman, but the man was belligerent and accusatory, and he got nowhere with him.

At length, though, he located some elders, and persuaded them to talk, and over many cups of tea he managed to persuade them that Thesiger was, in fact, an English traveller, merely passing through under the protection of the Emperor, and not a Government employee of any kind.

The elders decided that Omar and Thesiger should be taken to see their chief the next day to explain themselves, and that in the meantime they should retire to their camp for the night, and sleep. Or not, as the case might be. Or pace the perimeter, rifles in hand, shining battery-powered torches out into the darkness, hearts beating faster at every movement and each sound out there in the night.

But the next morning came, in the end, and the two men were taken a little way down the river, to a small village on the one dry patch of ground in a foul and malarious swamp, presided over by an ancient and mostly deaf chief by the name of Afleodham, who, it was said, was related to the Sultan of Aussa.

The meeting lasted throughout the day, not least because Afleodham could not hear the half of what was being said, most of the time, and had to have it repeated to him, several times over, which meant translating and retranslating in three languages; and all the while they were beset by great clouds of black flies from the swamp. It was not a wholesome sort of place to be.

Eventually, the chief pronounced himself satisfied with what he had heard, and agreed that Thesiger's party should be allowed to pass through his lands to Aussa, accompanied by an escort of Asaimara warriors.

Elated, Thesiger retired to his tent, and stayed there until just before sunset, when the letter from the regional government office arrived.

A Letter

The letter had been passed from village to village and from chief to chief, and was addressed not to Thesiger but to the head of his military escort.

It informed him that the Englishman, Wilfred Thesiger, was required to return immediately to Addis Ababa. He was under no circumstances to attempt to enter Bahdu or the land of Aussa that lay beyond. Should he refuse, the soldiers were to return without him, bringing all of their rifles and ammunition, and after first announcing to the Danakil that the authorities took no further responsibility for his safety.

And that, pretty much, was that.

Officialdom had taken its revenge good and proper, and, through a combination of conscious design and fortuitous circumstances, had served it up in exactly the way and at exactly the time most certain to destroy Thesiger's hopes, just at the moment when the possibility of eventual success had seemed to be within reach.

Such are the consequences of upsetting those in positions of authority.

So it was that the party set off on the return trip – this time to Afdam Station, which was nearer than Awash. The soldiers, it must be said, were really rather pleased, and Thesiger was somewhat less so – though determined, more than ever, to find a way to return and to enter Aussa.

The trip to the station took them four days. On the second day they arrived at a well in the dry bed of the Mullu River, a tributary of the Awash, by the side of which lay the charred remains of an Adoimara village, the bones of its inhabitants scattered around where the jackals had dragged them; and on the fourth day, when they arrived at the station, they heard, from local tribesmen, the story of what had happened there.

To the North

After an hour or so of walking another bus pulled up beside us, loud African music blaring from within. It was already packed to overflowing; packed both with its own passengers and with stragglers from our bus it had picked up on the way. Some people hung from the doors, some sat on others' laps. Some *chickens* sat on other chickens' laps, such was the press within.

And yet, somehow, we managed to climb on board.

We spent the night at a cheap hotel by Thompson's Falls, sleeping on the bare floorboards of a single room, which though it lacked the luxury of a working light-bulb, was nevertheless clean and well kept. And cheap.

Then we took breakfast at the big old colonial-era hotel nearby, eating toast and scrambled eggs and fresh fruit, all delicious and plentiful, and served up to us by attentive uniformed waiters. This also was remarkably cheap, and much to be recommended.

Greatly refreshed, we climbed down to the bottom of the falls and explored the dense forest by the river's edge, seeing the footprints of a big cat of some kind, before joining our next bus around lunchtime, bound for Thesiger's home town of Maralal, in the north.

For most of this journey we sat on the roof-rack of the bus, among the luggage, with the hot wind blowing in our faces, and we watched as the land spread out around us became ever flatter and more arid. There came a point at which the tarmac roads gave way to packed dirt. At this point also the appearance and manner of the people changed altogether, as if we had crossed a border and entered another country, where lived a different race. It was, this place, one of traditional people, of picture-book people: of women in bead collars; young girls in mother-of-pearl head-dresses; spear-carrying young men in bright red togas with ochred hair. And also the bearing of them, we noticed, the posture and the stance of them: very upright and very tall, and a look about them as if all they surveyed belonged to them and them alone.

We saw giraffes and herds of zebra, also; and at one point we had to stop while the driver got out and flapped his arms at two elephants, which were sitting in the road. On being approached, the beasts heaved themselves to their feet and lurched away, flapping their ears and casting looks over their shoulders as they went.

Maralal means 'glittering'.

It was so called because of the corrugated-iron roofs of the buildings in its single street, when they were built, of which no one in the area had ever seen the like before; and how they sparkled and glittered in the sun.

Crowds of children had gathered to watch the bus arrive. No sooner had we climbed down than we were surrounded by small boys in shorts, the uniform of the local mission school, wanting to know whether we had anything to give them – sweets, money or the like. Across the street, at a roadside trough, Samburu girls in traditional costume threw water at each other and ran and dodged to escape retaliation, shrieking with laughter.

After some time the crowds began to disperse, and a young Turkana man in Western dress approached us.

'I am Kibiriti,' he said, holding out his hand, 'You are Wilfred's guests, yes?'

We said that we were indeed.

'That is good,' he said. 'That is very good. We have been expecting you. Wilfred has been delayed, but he has made arrangements for you. He will be here to see you soon. But for now, you come to my house.'

Kibiriti

In Maralal, Wilfred Thesiger had three sons, Lawi, Laputa and Kibiriti.

They were not his sons in the biological sense, Thesiger never having married, but they were his sons in every other sense, since he had taken them up, as young orphans, and cared for them, and paid for their clothing and education. When they came to adulthood, he had set them up with homes and with cattle with which to buy wives, as was the custom of their tribes.

Kibiriti's house was a wattle-and-daub hut, iron-roofed, and it sat within a gated picket-fence, in the middle of a garden in which grew flowers and vegetables – the only garden of its kind in all of Maralal, he told us, proudly. He had got the idea from pictures of English houses shown to him by his adoptive father. The house was cool and surprisingly spacious inside, though simply furnished, and the walls of dried red mud were decorated all over with a pattern of white clay spots, and with framed black-and-white photographs of Thesiger.

We sat and drank tea, hot and sweet, and talked about our lives; and then Kibiriti prepared for us a huge and hugely filling meal. It had something of a theme to it: the theme was *goat*.

First came a plate of dried goat-meat nibbles, followed by a great bowl of goat with boiled rice. This was followed in turn by an even bigger platter of roasted goat meat.

It would have been very bad form, I think, and rude and ungrateful in the extreme, to mention the fact that back then I was – and still am, I ought to say – a vegetarian. That I was the sort of vegetarian who hadn't eaten meat or fish of any kind for many years; who would, as a matter of course, go out of his way to avoid stepping on an insect; who would never dream of wearing a leather jacket; just the sort of irritating, holier-than-thou vegetarian you would find it an absolute chore to cater for at a dinner-party. And a non-drinker, too. A bundle of fun, in fact.

I ate what I was given, though, fighting back the instinct to gag at the surprisingly gristly toughness of it – which was not at all how I remember the meat I ate as a child; and when I had finished I smiled and rubbed my stomach, and heaped the cook with praise.

I think I must have succeeded, to some extent, because when we finished Kibiriti smiled and winked at my companions and said, 'He likes his meat, this one – well, we will have a treat for him tomorrow!'

Upon the Etiquette of Massacre

In February 1692, a party of 120 soldiers of the first and second companies of the Earl of Argyll's Regiment of Foot, under the command of Captain Robert Campbell of Glenlyon, marched out from Fort William on the shores of Loch Linnhe, through the bleak winter landscape. Snow on the mountains and an icy wind blowing.

They crossed the water by boat at Ballachulish and then headed along the shores of Loch Leven for some sixteen miles, until they saw thin streams of smoke spiralling upwards in the bleak winter sky from the stone-hut village of the MacDonalds of Glencoe, which lay by the shore of the River Coe, beneath the mountainous ridge of Aonach Eagach, to the north, and, to the South, the twin peaks of Buachaille Etive Mor and Buachaille Etive Beag, the great and little shepherds of Etive.

They made their way to the house of the chief of that clan, whose name was MacIain, and there they were met by his sons, who came out to greet them.

The eldest son spoke out.

'Greetings, Robert Campbell,' he said, holding up his hand towards them. 'Do you come in war or in peace?'

'In peace,' said Campbell, 'from Fort William.'

'What brings you here to our village?'

'Building-work,' said Campbell, 'and the movement of men at the Fort.'

MacIain's son inclined his head for Campbell to continue.

'There have been new units admitted,' he said, 'and the old barracks are full. The new barracks are not yet ready, and we have been sent to quarter in Glencoe with your people.'

'You are welcome here,' said MacIain's son, though there was no love lost between the men, but Campbell had requested hospitality, and it was the custom in those parts that such requests could not be refused.

There had been much blood shed between the Campbells of Glenlyon and the MacDonalds of Glencoe over the years. Mostly it had been over questions of cattle theft and ownership of land and grazing rights. Not four years before, a party of Glencoe MacDonalds, together with their Glengarry cousins, had raided Robert Campbell's lands and stolen his livestock, putting him into debt and necessitating, incidentally, his decision to join the army for the wage it offered; but at this time they found themselves on opposite sides of something much bigger – something that was, in all respects, a civil war over the throne of Scotland.

With the ascendancy of William of Orange, all the Highland chiefs were required to swear an oath of loyalty to the Crown; and it had been judged that MacIain had been unduly slow and reluctant in doing so, and his loyalty was considered suspect, if not downright false.

With this in mind, Captain Campbell was dispatched to Glencoe with a very particular and most secret set of orders.

The MacDonalds welcomed Campbell's men into their homes as guests; and though Campbell himself was what he was, and who he was, and of the clan from which he came, he was also related to the MacDonald chief through marriage; and so he was given a bed in one of MacIain's own houses.

The soldiers were fed, housed and entertained for some two weeks, until the night of the twelfth. That night, Campbell spent the evening playing cards with his hosts, before wishing them goodnight and accepting an invitation to dine with them the following night.

But later, in the early hours of the following morning, a single shot rang out. It was a signal for which the soldiers had been waiting, dressed and armed; and upon the sound of it they turned upon their hosts, dragging them from their beds and slaughtering them in front of their homes.

In all, thirty-eight MacDonalds were killed by the soldiers. Another forty, mostly women and children, died of exposure in the snow after fleeing from their burning houses.

The number of deaths would have been higher still, were it not that the idea of killing one's host – of murder under trust – was considered deeply shameful in Highland culture. No matter how much you might happen to loathe a man, and no matter that, if you were to come across him in other circumstances, you would happily slit his throat as soon as look at him, it was just not the done thing to kill him while a guest under his roof.

For this reason, not all of the soldiers were wholly enthusiastic about their task, nor were they wholly diligent in carrying it out.

Some found ways of warning their hosts beforehand, saying things like 'If I were a sheep, I think I would head up to the hills tonight', while giving their hosts the kind of meaningful looks that either persuaded them that they had lost their marbles altogether, or else that they had some urgent message of the utmost importance to impart. Two lieutenants, Francis Farquhar and Gilbert Kennedy, went so far as to break their swords rather than carry out their orders, and for this were subsequently imprisoned for their disobedience – though they were pardoned at a later date.

The ruins of MacIain's house can still be seen to this day, in a wood not far from the present-day village of Glencoe, overgrown with heather and bracken.

More than 300 years later, people in those parts still sing of the massacre in ballads:

> Some died in their beds at the hand o' the foe
> Some fled in the night and were lost in the snow
> Some lived tae accuse him wha' struck the first blow
> But gone was the house of MacDonald.

And there is a story, also, of a soldier in Campbell's regiment who was sent down to search beneath the bridge of the River Coe, where it was believed that a number of the MacDonalds might be hiding. Sure enough, he found a small group of women and children huddled down there; but rather than kill them all, he drew his sword and, taking hold of the arm of one among them, a young boy, he cut off one of the boy's fingers, smearing the blood along the length of his blade, before returning to his unit to report his 'success'.

It is also told how many years later, as an old man, this same soldier passed through Glencoe once more on his way to conduct some business in Fort William. It was late and he was tired, and he stopped at the new inn in the rebuilt village, which is, as I say, a little way down from where the old one stood; and there he fell to drinking, and to thinking about what had gone before and what he had taken part in; and feeling burdened by the shame and guilt of it, he told his story to the innkeeper. Now, this man listened carefully, all the way through, and when at last the old soldier reached the end of his story he said nothing. Instead, he simply held up his hand, to reveal his missing finger.

I do not know if this is true or not; but that is the story as I heard it.

The story that Wilfred Thesiger heard of the events at the ruined Adoimara village by the Mullu River on his arrival Afdam Station was, in some ways, a remarkably similar one to the story of the MacDonalds of Glencoe; and yet, at the same time, it was very different indeed, and it revealed much about the culture of the Danakil peoples.

There had been trouble, as ever, between the Adoimara and the Asaimara, and at this particular time there had been a dispute over pasture rights on the plain by the river, and there had been fighting and people killed. It had gone on for some time, this dispute, and the casualties were mounting; and so in an effort to calm things somewhat, the Asaimara sent a deputation of seven old men to negotiate a truce with the elders of their rivals.

These old men were received with courtesy and with feasting, and were each given a bed in the homes of Adoimara elders.

And then, one night, upon a pre-arranged signal, the Adoimara hosts rose up, dragged their elderly guests from their beds and set about hacking them to death. They killed six of them, horribly. The seventh managed to escape, despite a shattered arm and deep wounds all over his body, and was able to reach his people and tell them what had happened.

A few days later the Asaimara descended on the village in force and in fury, laying waste to it and killing every single inhabitant – sixty-one men, women and children – and not sparing even the youngest baby among them.

The moral of the story being, presumably, you don't mess with the Asaimara.

The day after hearing the story, Thesiger took the train up to Addis Ababa, to see if anything could be done to save his expedition.

Preparations

We spent the night in a hut next to Kibiriti's, lying on our backs within the red mud walls listening to the sounds of girls and women singing long into the darkness.

It was the wedding season, after the rains.

One pays for a bride in livestock, Kibiriti had explained to us. Most brides are 'booked' many years before their wedding, when they are still very young; and in the years between, the men who are to be their husbands buy them as many bead necklaces as they can afford, to make their girls more beautiful than all the other girls.

Samburu girls from Maralal, he said, were notoriously expensive. He himself had just two brides. Due to the prohibitive cost of local girls, though, he had been forced to obtain them from other towns.

The next morning, Kibiriti collected us from our hut and took us into town.

'There is much to do,' he said.

The streets of Maralal were full of *moran*, young warriors with ochred hair, who loitered in groups, leaning on their spears.

The things that there were to do, he said, were to do with the arrangements that had been made for us to go out and see the countryside, while waiting for Wilfred to arrive.

Thus it was that we found ourselves standing in front of Mr Bhola's garage-cum-hardware store in Maralal.

'Rope,' said Kibiriti, 'you will need rope. And sacks. Many sacks.'

We couldn't see how or why we might need these things, but he seemed to know what he was doing and so we let him get on with it.

'And you will need water-containers.'

'Ahem . . .' said Frazer, holding up the two-pint British Army waterbottle he had clipped to his belt, 'We have waterbottles.'

'No,' said Kibiriti, 'these are not big enough. You will need these', and with this, Mr Bhola came out of his shop carrying a stack of large plastic jerry-cans, such as you might see bolted to the side of a jeep.

'These are good,' said Kibiriti.

'And pangas,' he said, at which Mr Bhola went into the back of the shop and came out carrying an armful of broad-bladed machetes.

'Five,' said Kibiriti.

Mr Bhola counted out five of the knives and put them down on the rapidly growing pile of provisions.

'Excuse me,' said Andy, 'but what will we need these for?'

'Protection,' Kibiriti said.

'And that would be protection from what, exactly?'

'It is nothing,' he said, 'just some Shifta.'

'Shifta?'

'Bad men.'

Frazer, Andy and I looked at each other.

'But it is not a problem,' Kibiriti continued, 'Chukana will come with you also. He has a Kalashnikov. Now, you will need to eat. We must have flour.'

And he then proceeded to buy four 20-pound sacks of maize flour. The sort of quantity we might want, say, if we were planning to open a bakery. Or if we were planning be quite a long way from bakeries and such things for quite some time. I had a suspicion it was going to be the latter, rather than the former.

Following on from the flour came large metal cooking-pots, large quantities of tea and sugar and also plugs of tobacco.

'We don't smoke,' said Frazer.

'They are to trade,' Kibiriti said, 'with the desert people. They are not familiar with paper money. Also you will need camels.'

These were not something that Mr Bhola stocked, nor was he able to supply the men skilled at handling them. For these, Kibiriti suggested we head out the next day to the wells at Ilaut, some sixty miles to the north, where the Rendille tribe watered their herds, and where we might engage the men and beasts we needed. From there, he said, we could load up our provisions and then start out on our walk.

'Where are we going to, exactly?' said Andy.

'Wilfred says that you would like to see the desert and Mount Kulal. Also Lake Turkana. And also the oasis at South Horr. These are places he visited many years ago, with camels.'

'I see,' I said, 'and about how far is it?'

It would be twenty miles, Kibiriti said.

It seemed a long way to walk in the heat, but I reckoned we could handle it.

'And the next day,' said Kibiriti, 'twenty miles also. And then twenty miles the next. Every day twenty miles. And when you finish, I will come to collect you.'

'Ah. I see. And how far will we be walking, altogether? Just out of interest.'

We would be walking somewhere on the far side of 200 miles.

The Worst Restaurant in the World

Once we had obtained our provisions, Kibiriti took us out in his brother Lawi's motor-car, a Toyota Land Cruiser.

It was not at all certain whether Lawi knew he had the car, or whether he would be happy if he did know.

It was, it seems, something of a sore subject with Kibiriti. And with Lawi also, but for different reasons.

'I would not take it so often,' said Kibiriti, 'but Wilfred will not buy me one.'

'No?'

'No.'

We drove on at some speed, bumping and rattling as we flew over the rutted track, the Toyota's suspension making grating and grinding noises whenever we hit a particularly big bump.

'He will not buy me one,' said Kibiriti, 'because he says I drive too fast.'

'Oh.'

And quite suddenly he veered from the track, slamming his foot on the accelerator and surfing the car across the sand and scrub. A large, prickly thorn bush seemed to be his chosen target, but before the car hit it a big flightless bird shot out from behind it, and Kibiriti put the car into a slide, flattening the bush as he swerved after it. The engine stalled and the bird made its escape.

'A pity,' said Kibiriti, watching it run off as he restarted the engine, 'These birds are very tasty.'

Several other sorties after other wildlife of various shapes and sizes met with a similar lack of success, and we ended up at a wooden hut several miles out of Maralal, outside which stood a rusty oil-drum on hot coals, in which bubbled a foul-smelling grey liquid with white froth upon it. By this drum, fly-encrusted goat entrails hung from hooks, drying in the sun. And beneath the entrails squatted an ancient and wrinkled woman, scrubbing white-eyed, fire-blackened goat heads with a wire brush.

As we climbed out of the car the woman rose and grinned, revealing her two remaining teeth. I was half-expecting her to hail one of us as Thane of Cawdor, but instead she ushered us inside, to where clusters of Samburu men sat around tearing at the chunks of boiled goat meat which were heaped on communal chopping-boards placed in the centre of the tables at which they sat.

Luckily, or indeed unluckily, a table had recently been vacated – as could be seen by the scraps of skin and bone left strewn all over the chopping-board and spilling onto the table, and by the flies that had gathered to share in these scraps. An old man motioned to us to sit down, upon which he brought handfuls of boiled goat to pile on top of the previous diners' leftovers. The old woman, meanwhile, brought us chipped enamel mugs filled to the brim with the steaming grey liquid from the drum.

Then both man and woman stood back, arms folded, to watch us tuck in.

Addis Ababa

Sir Sidney Barton was not known for displays of temper.

A lawyer by training, he disapproved of them, as a rule, and held them to be a sign of weakness in a man's argument. To lose one's temper, for him, was a sign that the other fellow held all the high cards in the game.

Since being appointed British Minister in Addis Ababa he had become known for his quiet diplomacy, his ability to have just the right words in just the right ears to make the wheels turn to achieve a satisfactory outcome.

And yet, faced with the stubbornness, the obduracy, the deafness to all reason of this man sitting implacably across the table from him, his fingers meshed in self-satisfaction across the front of his buttoned-up jacket, he felt the blood rushing to his face.

'Damn it all!' he exclaimed, rising to his feet and thumping the table with his fist. 'You *will* let him go. Or you won't hear the last of this from me.'

The Governor of Chercher Province inclined his head slightly to one side, closing his eyes for a moment before speaking.

'No. It is out of the question, I am afraid. Completely out of the question.'

'Do you realise,' said Sir Sidney, 'quite how much money has been invested in this venture? Not the least of it by your own Emperor.'

'That may well be the case. But circumstances change. As, indeed, they have. It is a dangerous place at the best of times, and if I were you I would hesitate to allow this young man' – he nodded towards Thesiger, who sat, tense and alert, at the end of the table – 'to travel in such a place even then – and to put not just his own life at risk, but the lives of his companions with him. But you cannot fail to be aware of the present situation in Bahdu. In such circumstances it would be little short of suicidal—'

'But sir,' interjected Thesiger, 'I have assurances from the Asaimara.'

The Governor gave a little snort.

'So you say,' he said, 'and it might be interesting, perhaps, to see what these "assurances" would amount to in practice. But you will not have that opportunity. This is my final word on the matter.'

He rose to his feet.

'And now,' he said, 'if you two gentlemen will excuse me, I have pressing business to attend to.'

'Very well,' said Sir Sidney. 'If that is your word, then we must respect it.'

'I am glad that we agree on this. Good day, gentlemen.'

'And no doubt,' Sir Sidney continued, 'you are well aware of your personal contractual obligations for having permitted the expedition to begin, and costs to be incurred, and then cancelling your permission. But this is something we can return to at a later date, when you have more time . . .'

Chukana is Indisposed

We engaged Chukana, the man with the Kalashnikov and the knowledge of the way across the desert to the north, and we paid him a thousand Kenyan shillings, his wages in full and in advance.

On the next day, however, the day of our departure for Ilaut, Kibiriti returned from Chukana's hut with a worried look on his face.

Chukana was unwell, he said, and indisposed.

He was this way on account of being blind drunk, having converted his entire wages into alcohol and downed the lot the previous night.

He would be going nowhere in a hurry, said Kibiriti, except to vomit.

Although, he said, he had not even bothered to move to do that, judging by the state of his hut: it seemed that he preferred, in his current state, to roll over and do it where he lay. Or not even to roll over, come to think of it.

But on a positive note, he said, he had managed to obtain the services of another guide – and a cook – at short notice. This guide was Chukana's cousin, a young man called Osman, and the cook went by the name of Leleruk, as I recall. Between them, they would only want 800 shillings, partly on account of neither of them having a Kalashnikov – or indeed any kind of a gun. And partly, also, on account of the fairly rudimentary nature of Leleruk's cooking skills. But at least Osman knew the way.

'And the Shifta?' I said.

Apparently, in recent months, bands of Shifta had been crossing the Somali border. They had killed two people in the desert two weeks before, and robbed several more.

'This is not a problem,' said Kibiriti, 'the Rendille will be armed.'

I did ask what it was that the Rendille would be armed with, exactly, but he was somewhat vague on the details, and answered with a sort of wave of the hand.

'We must leave,' he said, 'there is much to do.'

We drove north; and as we drove the land became ever flatter and ever hotter.

From time to time we passed small villages, some the pointed-roofed huts of the Samburu and others the domed, skin-covered 'igloos' of the Turkana and Rendille peoples.

Like the Samburu, the Turkana and the Rendille have their own distinctive manner of dress.

Turkana men wear their hair pulled back into a 'bun' which is caked in clay and painted, so that it takes on the appearance of a decorated coconut-shell, while the women shave only the sides of their heads, weaving the remaining crest into patterns of tiny plaits.

The Rendille, both male and female, are less flamboyant than their neighbours, many wearing only cloth or skin 'skirts' – and beads for women – and being naked from the waist up.

We saw ostriches, and tiny deer known as dik-dik, as we bounced and clattered along the road, which had become, by now, no more than a vague shadow of a trail among the sand and scrub and scattered rocks, until at last we reached the herders' settlement of Ilaut, where we unpacked our provisions and made camp by the side of one of the main goat highways.

'Tomorrow,' said Kibiriti, 'we will have camels. And Rendille.'

The Water-Song and the Camel-Men

In the morning we went with Kibiriti to the wells to look for men who might go with us across the desert.

We heard the wells before we saw them: a hypnotic, melodic droning sound which I took, at first, for some strange chance effect, a fortuitous harmonic combination of the deep, contented lowing of the hundreds upon hundreds of sheep and goats that clustered around the stone troughs that stood by a deep hole or void in the ground.

As we approached, however, we realised that the sound was coming from beyond the animals, from the hole itself; and as we reached it we looked down to see a wide, deep hole stretching many feet down into the ground, down into darkness, and the walls were cut up at the side into rough steps, upon which stood a long human chain of Rendille, passing tin buckets of water from hand to hand from the dark depths, and chanting as they worked.

The chant was an endless repetition, with variations, of two syllables, over and over again. One man made a long, deep 'nnn' sound, to which all the others replied with a sort of nasal vowel sound; or that was the constant basis of their response, but on top there was change and fluctuation as men mixed in other sounds and voices, and as the buckets came up and the clear water was poured into the troughs. And the animals clustered around, drinking their fill, and the empty buckets were passed down, hand over hand, and constantly replaced with full ones passed up from below. And it was the sound of life, the sound that signified life and was life, and that brought life into the barren land, and sustained life when all else around was emptiness.

A cup was passed to us and we each drank from it, Frazer, Andy, Kibiriti and me, and it was cool and fresh, and tasted of the earth.

And later that morning, Kibiriti came back to our camp by the goat highway followed by two Rendille, leading three camels.

'This is Apa,' said Kibiriti, motioning to the elder of the two Rendille. 'He will take you across the desert. He does not speak English, but Osman speaks his language. He can translate for you.'

We shook hands.

Apa did not have a gun, but both he and his companion carried spears. With which, no doubt, you can bat Shifta bullets out of the way if you're quick enough.

'And this is his cousin,' said Kibiriti, and we all shook hands with the younger Rendille.

I noticed them both giving Andy something of a queer look as he offered his hand, and also exchanging glances when they heard him talking to us in English.

'These are Apa's camels,' said Kibiriti, somewhat unnecessarily, for we had a pretty good idea of what they were and of whom they might belong to. We did not shake hands with them.

A short while later, Kibiriti went off and returned with a *moran* leading a goat. He did not introduce either the man or the goat, but I had a feeling that this goat was, or had recently become, our personal goat, and that we were soon to become rather better acquainted with it than I might perhaps have wished, given the choice.

Upon Human Nature, and Goats

Once, a few years ago, I had been out cycling.

I had, at that time, an enormously expensive – and uninsured – mountain-bike, and I came home with it on a rack on the roof of my car. Because my mother was visiting, and because I had absented myself, leaving her, and my wife and children, for several hours, I came straight in, leaving the bike still on the car. I had not been indoors for more than a few minutes when we heard a loud banging sound from outside, and footsteps running away. I ran out into the street to find that the bike had been ripped from the roof by three young men, one of whom had ridden off on it, and the other two of whom were running after him.

I set off in pursuit.

My wife ran to the phone and began to call the police, only for my mother, a small woman born and raised in the East End of London, to clamp her finger down on the phone cradle.

'My Warwick can handle himself,' she said. Or words to that effect.

The two young men, meanwhile, were off at full pelt, and for perhaps a quarter of a mile I could not gain on them, nor they on me, until all of a sudden, and simultaneously, we all seemed

95

to hit a physical 'wall' and all slowed, coughing and panting, to a walking pace.

But I gathered my breath, and put everything into one last sprint, catching up with them just as I was almost completely done for. One was smaller than me; the other bigger, and so I grabbed the smaller one around the neck and choked him, while telling the other one to use his mobile phone to call the third back, and the bike with him.

He did not do so.

There were, besides, two of them and only one of me; but because we had all exhausted ourselves in the running there followed something of a stand-off, in which none of us did anything for perhaps five or ten minutes.

And then, all of a sudden, the bigger one came at me. I let the other one go – he ran off instantly – and the two of us grappled. I tried to grab him around the neck: he bit my hand, and so I grabbed his shirt with my other hand and then began punching him in the face as hard as I could.

At this point some passers-by came and pulled us apart.

'Break it up, you two,' they said.

'But he's stolen my bike,' I said, as my fingers were prised away from his shirt.

'What bike?' they said

Exactly.

Upon which the young man took to his heels and disappeared, and I never saw him or the bike again.

But here's a thing: there was, I found, an exhilaration in punching the young man, an intense pleasure in it, in the feeling of contact and recoil, in the repeated smack of my knuckles against his face, and in the joyful and sincere hope that I had broken his nose or at least loosened a couple of teeth.

I feel it a compensation for my loss even now.

I feel this far more so than if he had been caught by the police and cautioned or fined, or sentenced to a few hours' community service, or else sent on some sort of course to 'rehabilitate' him.

And I know that if I were ever to see him again, even now, all these years later, I would do everything within my power to put him in hospital.

This is how I feel, and I would be a liar to pretend otherwise.

A while back I was reading a book called *Quartered Safe out Here*, by George MacDonald Fraser, the author of the Flashman books. The book is a memoir of his military service in the East, during the Second World War; and there comes a point, about halfway through, where he describes how he felt when, in fierce close combat around an enemy bunker, he shot and killed a man, shortly after one of his own comrades was himself shot down:

> I turned to see a Jap racing across in front of the bunker, a sword flourished above his head. He was going like Jesse Owens, screaming his head off, right across my front; I just had sense enough to take a split second, traversing my aim with him before I fired; he gave a convulsive leap, and I felt a jolt of delight – I'd hit the bastard!

'A jolt of delight': the phrase stops you dead in your tracks.

He returns to the same incident again, a few pages on:

> Putting a grenade into a bunker had the satisfaction of doing grievous bodily harm to an enemy for whom I felt real hatred, and still do . . . but seeing Gale go down sparked something which I felt in the instant when I hung on my aim at the Jap with the sword, because I wanted to be sure. The joy of hitting him was the strongest emotion I felt that day.

*   *   *

There was once an extraordinarily prolific mass murderer, in England, by the name of Harold Shipman. This Shipman was a doctor, and it was his habit, and his pleasure, to kill off the elderly and vulnerable among his patients, for their inheritances and also for other reasons best known to himself. Over the years he managed to finish off well over 200 people. Eventually, he was caught; and when he was caught, this Doctor Shipman, he showed not the slightest concern or remorse. Instead, he showed peevish irritation at those who had caught him, and annoyance that they had the audacity to ask him to explain himself; and, frankly, he was having none of it. Eventually, when it became apparent to him that he was going to have to spend the rest of his life in prison, and that he would be expected to conform to all of the accompanying rules and regulations, he ripped up his bedsheets, tied one end to the bars of his cell window and hung himself, dead.

And bloody good riddance to him, you might say; and a shame he didn't do it sooner; and more of a shame still that the law didn't do it for him, at a time and in a place set down by the court, whether he liked it or not.

And so you – or at least I – might expect anyone of sound mind to say.

So it was that the then-Home Secretary, a man by the name of David Blunkett, when asked for his response to the news of Shipman's death, told journalists: 'You wake up and you receive a phone call telling you that Shipman has topped himself . . . Then you have to think for a minute . . . is it too early to open a bottle?'

A perfectly natural and uncontroversial point of view, you might think: but not a bit of it, apparently. Instead, Blunkett found himself at the centre of an absolute storm of condemnation, with pretty much the whole of the political and media establishment lining up to give him a good kicking for his 'shameful irresponsibility', for owning up to feeling anything other than concern at the death of a mass-murderer, and demanding that he resign forthwith.

When it comes to retribution, some of us are Hamlet, endlessly agonising and debating over it, while some are more Laertes, driven viscerally towards it.

I know which side I fall down on.

'But let him come,' says Laertes, 'It warms the very sickness in my heart/ That I shall live and tell him to his teeth/ "Thus didest thou."'

I know how you feel: I understand.

It's the way I am. But it may not be the way you are.

People are different, I think: innately so and perhaps unalterably so.

I have read of research that says that identical twins are extraordinarily alike in just about any way you can measure, and that this is so whether they are raised together or apart, even when each is unaware of the other's existence. And it says that unrelated children raised together as brothers and sisters turn out no more similar in personality tests than they would if they had never even met – no matter what kind of upbringing they had. Or so they say.

They also say that you can tell a lot about a man's character and intelligence by the kinds of music he listens to. According to a study at the California Institute of Technology, devotees of Beethoven and, surprisingly, Heavy Metal are right up there at the brainbox end of the spectrum, while the fans of R&B, chart dance music and someone called Lil Wayne, apparently, are way down at the other. Thesiger didn't go in for music, much, as a rule, although he did tend to become rather cross at the idea of Michael Jackson. Me, on the other hand, I find myself greatly comforted by the moral wisdom of Country & Western ballads, and increasingly so as I become older. Songs like 'Coward of the County', for example, by Kenny Rogers, which teaches us that while, on the whole, it is a very bad thing to go around committing acts of violence for no particular reason, or for reasons base and dishonourable, and while it is a way of life that may see you ending your days in prison, leaving the care of your ten-year-old son, should you have one, to your brother, with the injunction that this child should never, at any cost, even think of doing the things you done; yet nevertheless there are some offences so rank and gross that they cry out to heaven for vengeance, and in these instances the only right and proper course of action for the wronged party is to seek immediate physical redress, irrespective of the odds, and irrespective of the harm that may befall him in the process. 'Sometimes,' as the song sagely observes, 'you got to fight to be a man.'

But the goat, which the *moran* led towards us by the horns, had done me no wrong.

Perhaps if, at some point, as I had bent to tie my shoelace, it had butted me up the backside, I might have felt differently.

Or perhaps if it had just bitten me a couple of times or something, or even just looked at me in an unpleasant way.

But I doubt it, somehow.

Apa and his cousin held the animal down.

The *moran* pulled out a long double-bladed knife from his scabbard and drew it across the animal's neck, severing its throat.

Then they let it go, upon which it kicked and struggled to its feet for a few moments before collapsing to its knees.

It tried to get up again, but fell again, this time landing heavily on its front knee and rolling over to one side, swinging its head back to reveal the full extent of the gaping wound.

Once more it tried to get up, but could not do so, and instead lay kicking and writhing in the dust until, at last, the kicking gave way to a sporadic twitching and then, with one final shudder, it lay still.

The creature was then swiftly skinned and butchered, and the liver, kidneys and stomach cooked over a fire and shared among us.

I managed to get down my share of the liver and kidneys, which tasted somewhat better than the goat meat we had eaten thus far. But I think you must need special teeth or something for eating stomach, because try as I might I could not bite through it. It was like trying to eat pieces of car-tyre.

So it was that I hit upon what seemed at the time to be a perfect way to dispose of this stomach without looking like a squeamish Westerner who couldn't handle the food: I flicked it behind me when I thought no one was looking.

It would have worked, too – were it not for the huge vultures that swooped down, landing screeching and squabbling right behind where I sat, fighting it out among themselves, at full volume, for the meat I had discarded. That, I think, might have been a bit of a giveaway.

Once we had eaten, we loaded up the camels and headed out into the scrubland that bordered the desert proper.

Kibiriti waved us off.

'I will meet you in South Horr,' he said.

A Question of Responsibility

It was, on many levels, the question of responsibility that was the sticking-point.

Responsibility, and who had it.

The Emperor was away, for one thing. This put the responsibility squarely upon the shoulders of the Governor, who was faced then, on the one hand, with the possibility of the violent death or otherwise of the Englishman and his Abyssinian escort, and its accompanying implications for the politics of Aussa and the balance of power within his province. And on the other hand there was Sir Sidney Barton and his incessant lawyerly insinuations regarding liability, and whether Bahdu should have been declared closed to the expedition right from the start, before arrangements were made and costs incurred.

And in all the weeks that these deliberations were in process there lived, in captivity, in another part of Addis Ababa, a man called Miriam Muhammad. Miriam Muhammad was the *Hangadaala*, the spiritual leader of the Asaimara Danakil of Bahdu. He was a Mohammadan, this Hangadaala, but his remit went some way beyond the strictures of his holy book. He was responsible, among other things, for bringing rain to the lands of his people, using powers obtained in the ceremony of his investiture.

In this ceremony, which had been handed down for generation after generation since way back before the memory of his people, he was woken at dawn and given a red cloth and a white cloth, in which he was dressed, and then he was smeared in ghee and lifted into a special throne. Four men then picked up the throne, each carrying his own assigned corner, which – like the role of the givers of the red cloth and the white – was hereditary. These four men then carried the Hangadaala some 200 yards from his home and set him down facing the rising sun, and then brought him back again, where his throne was placed on a bed before his house. In this position, crowds gathered round, among them representatives of all the clans of the Asaimara, and watched as earth from the top of Mount Ayelu was rubbed on his hands, clay from the bottom of the Awash River rubbed on his forehead and earth from under a big *shoal* tree was rubbed on his feet.

Quantities of ghee were then poured over him and his clothes, which was the signal for the assembled crowd to gather round and jostle and tussle for the privilege of touching him.

This being done, there were led into his presence four beasts: a red goat and a white one, and a red bull and a white one. The red bull first was lifted up over the Hangadaala's head and its throat cut, so that the animal's dying blood gushed out and ran down over him. Then the red goat followed. The Hangadaala's nearest relative then cut the throats of the white bull and the white goat, and the people of his clan rubbed themselves with the blood.

Then the men, next the women and finally the children of all the Asaimara clans crowded around to pour yet more ghee all over him.

The ceremony being complete, a hundred sheep were killed and eaten in celebration, and much milk was drunk, while the skins of the sacrificial bulls and goats were taken away to be dried for the Hangadaala to sleep on – all apart from the skins of the legs, which were given to the bearers of the throne.

In consequence of all this, Miriam Muhammad had the power, it was believed, and the responsibility, to bring rain to Bahdu, even on a clear and cloudless day.

And he was also believed, in certain official quarters, to have the power and responsibility, by the fact of his captivity in the capital, to hold his tribe back from outright rebellion. Although this power did not seem to be working particularly well at that time.

But two things happened, at last, to bring something of a change in the situation. One was that Thesiger wrote and signed a letter, drafted by Barton, absolving the Abyssinian authorities of all responsibility for the safety of his expedition and accepting all costs, consequences and eventualities upon himself.

The second thing that happened was that a suggestion was made that Miriam Muhammad be released to accompany Thesiger into Bahdu, as a gesture of goodwill from the provincial authorities to the Asaimara – and on the understanding that the Asaimara would reciprocate by paying, once more, the tribute demanded of them.

So it was that on 8th February 1934, Wilfred Thesiger once more set off from Awash Station, with his camels and his Somali camel-men and with a freshly picked but equally reluctant escort of fifteen Abyssinian soldiers. Four days later, accompanied by Omar the headman and Miriam Muhammad, he made his way once more through the narrow pass into the territory of Bahdu and made his camp there by the river's edge.

The Great Explorer

It is to my eternal shame that I say this, but I lasted for three hours.

I do not know how it can come to be that a young man in his twenties, in good health and carrying no baggage other than a small waterbottle, can walk for no more than three hours before feeling weak and dizzy, and before having an overpowering urge to sit down, but that is how I felt and I am not proud of it.

Andy – now, he had the build and the look of the people of those parts: tall and lean and high cheek-boned, and with his head shaved as well. Put him in local dress and you'd be hard-pushed to tell him from a Kenyan, apart from a slightly paler skin – but that was darkening anyway, the longer he was out in the sun. You might say that he had it in his genes, that he was built for the country, and perhaps some of his ancestors came from that part of the world, or somewhere similar. But that does not explain my brother, who looks pretty much as I do, in size and build and complexion; and after walking for three hours he seemed exactly as you would expect for someone who had walked that far: he'd worked up something of an appetite, as I recall.

Me, I felt faint, and strange, and off-balance, and not altogether there.

My brother offered me a mouthful of water, which I took, thirstily, and then promptly vomited back up.

For the next half an hour I lay on the ground beneath a small thorn bush, moving my head only to take occasional tiny sips of water – I could not hold more than a mouthful down; and then, after a while, some hot, sweet tea, which the others made for me.

I walked on afterwards, but very feebly, a step at a time and leaning upon a walking-stick as I went, stopping every hour to rest for some ten minutes. For people used to walking steadily all day, as Osman and our Rendille were, and with a commission to lead us for the next 200-odd miles over land that was to become hotter and drier still, this must have seemed a poor start indeed; but I could do no other, and so the day went on, slowly, slowly, until the sun went down over the horizon, when all of a sudden I felt a great hunger and a tremendous burst of the most manic energy.

The change that came over me then, with the setting of the sun, was such that I swear I almost checked my neck for puncture-marks and my canine teeth for signs of unusual elongation.

That night we ate a stew of dried goat and *ugali*, which is boiled maize-flour, together with some potatoes and vegetables. We shared these things with an old Rendille woman and her daughter who had appeared at our camp, dressed all in skins. Later, Apa cut a walking-stick from a thorn bush for Andy, who lacked one, and straightened and hardened it over the fire. They seemed to have a name for Andy, the Rendille; or some words they seemed to use when they were talking about him. I asked Osman what they called him, and he just smiled.

'It is nothing,' he said, 'it is just some words in their language.'

'But meaning what?'

Osman thought about it for a moment.

'They call him the black white man,' he said.

I went to Bombay, once, on business, with two British-born Indians, a man and a woman. The man was a regular visitor and he came from a wealthy family with property there, and servants and a driver. The woman had never been before. She was brought up speaking only English, and she spoke it with a broad West Yorkshire accent. Bradford, or thereabouts. She had been educated at an English university, up North, and had become something in marketing, and had moved down to London. She had two brothers and a sister, two doctors and a corporate lawyer, and her parents, second-generation immigrants born of Indian villagers who came to England in the last days of the Empire, had kept a corner-shop and had worked all hours to give their children the best start in life. She had cousins still in India, she said, but could hardly remember the last time she met them. She had been a small child when they had visited, and had been unable to speak their language or they to speak hers.

It was the end of the monsoon when we went, and we travelled the city in a motor-rickshaw, passing streets where women hitched up their saris and men their trousers, shoes tied together at the laces and hung around their necks to wade through water up to their knees, and still the rain came down, slantwise. Past sodden roadside shanties of cardboard and tarpaulin we went, weaving and swerving on the potholed tarmac, in and out of the heavy traffic when we could move, though for much of the time we were stuck in jams, eye-level with grease-encrusted lorry axles, and shuddering corroded exhaust-pipes that pumped black diesel-smoke into our faces, while beggars thrust mottled fingerless hands through the window-flaps at us.

We drove down roads of huge walled houses where the rich lived, outside which teams of Untouchable women swept dirt from the gutters with palm-fronds; and on through business districts and a street where the flow of suited men on their way to work parted to avoid a naked and skeletal sadhu rolling over and over on his side. Incense and prayer wafted from temples to many-limbed gods and goddesses, and music blared from the rickshaw-driver's transistor radio.

The size and scale and strangeness of the place took the woman's breath away as much as they did mine.

'But,' she said, pronouncing the word Yorkshire-style, 'but when I'm here, the world suddenly makes sense to me. That's the only way I can describe it. It just makes sense.'

'How's that?' I said.

'I don't know,' she said. 'I've never lived here. I couldn't live here. But when I walk down the street and everyone looks like me, it just feels . . . well, as I say, it feels like the world makes sense.'

Thesiger never thought of himself as anything but an Englishman, though he had no great love of the place itself.

'I find the English countryside dull,' he said, 'and uninteresting. I mean, you're not exactly going to come face-to-face with a rhinoceros there, are you?'

I would have asked Andy then what it felt like to be a 'black white man' from South London among black black men from Africa. Or rather, I don't know if I would have asked him, but I wonder now how I would have felt in his position. Would the world have made sense to me, at last?

Or were they as foreign to him as they were to me?

I wonder how deep the ancestral ties go. I wonder what it means to arrive, for the first time in your life, in a place where the people all look the way you look.

We slept the night by the cooking-fire, with a cool breeze blowing across our faces and the camels bedded down in a thorn-bush kraal.

A Blessing

The next day we rose just before dawn. In the cool of the early morning, while the camels were being loaded, Frazer and I set off together to make up for time lost the previous day.

'Let's go now,' he said, as we got out of our sleeping-bags. 'Get going before the sun's properly up. That way if it hits you like it did yesterday, we'll have covered a lot of distance before it does.'

'Good idea,' I said.

And it was.

Brothers.

Magnetic fields of relationship shifting and readjusting.

Me, I'm the eldest.

Frazer, he's good at competitive sports.

I do non-competitive ones, mostly. I've always tended to lose, and lose quite badly, whenever I've tried the other sort.

'We need to cover the miles,' he said.

As we left, the old Rendille woman rushed out from her camp, which was a little way from ours, and took our hands, holding them up and spitting on each of our open palms in turn.

This, Osman told us later, is considered a blessing among the Rendille.

We walked for an hour at a time, heading for a distant line of low trees that Osman had pointed out to us, pausing for ten minutes or so every hour to take a little water from our bottles; and in this way we covered a lot of ground before the real heat of the day.

Andy caught up with us after a couple of hours and we walked together, seeing a pair of giraffes and numerous antelope.

Antelope, by the way, is the plural form of 'antelope'.

And, indeed, the singular. It just is. Some words are like that.

I used to think it was *anteloe*.

'Home, home on the range,' was what it sounded like, in the song, 'where the deer and the anteloe play.' And also, from the same song, I learnt that the word 'seldom', when spoken in that particular place, had a uniquely discouraging effect. 'Where seldom is heard a discouraging word.'

I didn't actually know, at that time, what 'seldom' meant. Or discouraging, either. But I understood the currents of relationship between them, at least.

Or at least I thought that I did.

I wonder sometimes how much of what I know is like that.

Wrongly intuited, I think the expression is.

And how much of what I believe.

The answer is, I just don't know.

I don't think any of us do; except, perhaps in retrospect.

Except, perhaps, in wonderment at what we see as the monumental wrongheadedness of the unspoken assumptions of previous generations. How could they have believed such things? Done such things? What were they *thinking of*?

And even then, perhaps we only think we know.

'The truth is great,' as Coventry Patmore's poem goes, 'and shall prevail, When none cares whether it prevail or not.'

And I picture the wash of water against stones at the water's edge, beneath the overarching sky. Absence and emptiness.

Just before midday we reached the trees, which marked the edge of a dry river-bed. The leaves were green and gave shade, and we waited beneath them for the camels to join us.

When they reached us we ate a lunch of dried goat, and sat drinking sweet tea while the camels grazed. By 'sweet' I mean sweet as in a bag containing about a pound of sugar being emptied into the saucepan and stirred around to make a kind of viscously delicious syrup – that kind of sweet, rather than 'actually, I take two teaspoons' which passes for sweet among normal people where I live, or 'would you mind putting five in mine, missus?' which passes for sweet among builders.

After lunch we set off again, but all together this time – not least because the grass and bushes around the river-bed were a known haunt of lions. Or lion.

I think that the jury is out on the correct plural form of the word; but for Wilfred Thesiger it was always *lion*. Except that he pronounced it *laahn*.

Upon leaving this place, we crossed into land that became rapidly and markedly hotter, drier and more sparsely vegetated as we went.

The next water, we were told, was several days away, at a camp used by various tribes and their herds.

The Hangadaala Takes a Walk

Several days further on, they made their camp beneath two trees by the edge of a low river-cliff on the plain by the side of the Awash River, where crocodiles basked in great numbers in the water below. There the Asaimara found them, and came in large numbers to welcome Miriam Muhammad back to his country and his people.

They brought and killed two oxen, and Thesiger's party caught a dozen large catfish, and a great spread was set out in the Hangadaala's honour, while some twenty men formed a circle, shoulder to shoulder, and performed a *janili* dance, clapping their hands and chanting to a varying rhythm, and invoking the powers of the *janili*, a man renowned as a soothsayer. This man rose to his feet and entered the circle, where he stood on a sheepskin laid out for him and he covered his mouth and eyes with his *shamma,* or shawl. The chanting grew louder and the clapping faster, but none moved their feet, although all the dancers bent further and further forward. Then, quite suddenly, the *janili* began to speak, out loud, in a voice quite unlike his own; and at this the clapping and the chanting instantly stopped.

Slowly, very slowly, he raised his right arm, a finger outstretched, and pointed directly to where Thesiger sat.

All eyes turned to the Englishman.

'God speaks to me of this man,' said the *janili*.

'God speaks to me of this man,' chanted the dancers.

'This man, this foreigner who has entered, unbidden, the lands of the Asaimara . . .'

'This man,' the dancers repeated, 'this foreigner . . .'

The soldiers surreptitiously checked their rifles. Each of the fifteen of them had been issued by the Government with just fifteen bullets each.

There were, by now, several hundred Asaimara in the camp, all waiting to hear what the *janili* had to say.

The mathematics were not favourable.

'God,' said the *janili*, as the dancers echoed his words, 'has sent this man to us. He has brought us back our Hangadaala. He has averted for us a great trouble with the Government. But for his visit, they would have come and fought with us. Let us welcome him into our land. And let us conduct him safely onto his destination.'

And with this he turned back to the circle and the clapping and chanting began once again.

Later on Thesiger was introduced to a much-scarred old man who had been shot in the upper arm above the elbow and the bone shattered, and who had, besides, several spear wounds, all of which were in the process of healing. This man, he was told, was the sole survivor of the deputation of old men recently sent to the Adoimara, the deputation who had been welcomed with singing and dancing, feasted and then set upon. He had, perhaps, heard the story?

He had.

Not that the Asaimara had any intention of doing any such thing to Thesiger or to his party in this case, he was hastily reassured; for had he not brought them their Hangadaala? And for as long as Miriam Muhammad remained free, and safe and sound, then for that long would they be welcomed and given all possible assistance to ease their passage to Aussa.

Thus it was that that night, in the dead of night, after the feasting and the dancing, after the *janili*'s prophecies and the meeting with the massacre-survivor, Miriam Muhammad decided to leave Omar's tent, in which he had been staying, and to take a walk in the cool night air.

Deep Water

Perhaps it was to do with Miriam Muhammad's powers to find and bring water to his land; perhaps it was to do with the lateness of the hour, or the darkness round about; or the befuddling of his senses by age or by the excesses of feasting, but whatever the reason, he walked straight from the tent and over the edge of the river-cliff, falling fifteen feet down and landing with a splash in the deep waters of the Awash, waking the lazy crocodiles on the river's edge, which, sensing prey, dragged themselves down into the water and began to make their way towards him.

The Hangadaala came to the surface and called out, splashing with his hands and feet as he tried to outswim the beasts.

The noise alerted the Abyssinian sentries, who, rushing over to see what the commotion was, and realising who had fallen, and the consequences for them all if he were to be eaten, dived in and dragged him out, just as the crocodiles were almost upon him.

The next day, Miriam Muhammad announced that he no longer intended to travel onto Aussa, as had originally been planned. Instead, he would go to his home village, a few miles away, and remain there.

Nothing that could be said would persuade him otherwise.

But he wished Thesiger and his party the very best of luck.

In the Midday Sun

The sun climbed high into the sky over the barren land; and as it did so, so my strength left me; and with my strength my spirit also, and I felt a great weight of depression upon my shoulders, and a sense of pointlessness and worthlessness.

My throat was drier than I had ever known it, and sore and ulcerated with it. We had little water between us, and thirst was constant and all-consuming, and besides what we carried there was no more to be had until we reached the wells. Each hour I allowed myself a small mouthful from my bottle, but it did little to help.

The walking, meanwhile, was monotonous and endless on these days: hour after hour with no shade and little to be seen but sand and stones and the occasional low thorn bush.

I had begun, also, to lose my appetite, particularly in the heat of the day. All I wanted was water, cool water, and I could find no pleasure in food, nor any point in trying to get it down.

As a result I began to lose weight, and to lose it quite dramatically. Each day I would wake up noticeably thinner than the day before, so that my shorts, which had fitted at the start, began to hang on me and I had to tighten my belt by a notch at a time, sometimes twice in a day.

A Collective Decision

For reasons that he could not fathom, Thesiger had been sick all that night, violently sick, and the tent reeked of it.

He was awakened by a soldier at the tent-flap, calling his name.

He had been calling his name for some time, this soldier, and also prodding at his foot.

He rolled over and pulled his covers around him, calling to the man to go away and to come back later.

The soldier half-turned as if to do so but two others behind him nudged him in the back and pointed into the tent. There was a brief, urgently whispered conversation between them with a number of gesticulations, and then the first soldier knelt down and put his head through the tent door.

He apologised for any inconvenience he might be causing. However, there were important matters that needed to be mentioned, and changes to the situation to be taken into account. He was speaking on behalf of the entire company, who had discussed the matter at some length and all come to a collective decision, which they were quite certain about.

It was, he said, to do with the matter of Miriam Muhammad.

This matter was problematic, in terms of the guaranteeing of safe passage, and the passing through hostile territory with – as the gentleman himself knew – no more than fifteen rounds per head. Which was not many – not many at all. Being a shooting man himself, the gentleman would no doubt be all too aware of that fact. And all things considered, it would be best not to continue with the expedition, under the present circumstances, but perhaps to go home and come back another time, when Miriam Muhammad had changed his mind.

Either way, he said, the soldiers had decided among themselves that they would proceed no further, and that was their final word on the matter.

Built for Miserable Weather

One day we set off around dawn, as we always did; but as we walked on through the morning the sun did not rise as it had before – or rather, it did, but the sky was overcast and the weather cool, and grey clouds began to gather, low in the sky.

The darker and more slate-grey the sky became, the more my mood lifted and the more I felt the energy and the enthusiasm flooding back into me. I found that when I walked I did not get tired, as I had before; nor did my head feel light and dizzy or my throat sore; and everything, even the sand, seemed to take on a new fascination.

Even the constant raging thirst of the desert, and the meagre supplies of water we carried with which to quench it, seemed matters of little consequence; opportunities, rather, to talk endlessly about the lemon sorbets we would consume when we went home, and the glasses of ice-cube lemonade and suchlike.

What were those tracks? What made this bush lean so, when there was no wind?

And also food, and what was for lunch, and indeed for dinner?

Dried goat and *ugali*, was it? Who would have thought?

But beggars, as they say, cannot be choosers.

Now, onward.

I am built for miserable weather, I think.

I think that I am built for grey skies and for drizzle, and for the rain plastering my hair to my forehead and dripping off my nose onto sodden clothes.

And the soft earth and the smell of woodland, also, and the mossy pools by the wayside.

I remember.

I remember, once, the foot of a wooded bank, and the ground deep in autumn leaves, russet and yellow, and sitting still, very still, and hearing a rustle and a commotion among the leaves a little way up, and a woodmouse, it was, came scurrying down, and lost its footing and rolled, once, twice, three times, to land at my feet. It shook itself, and looked up at me. Black eyes, like small beads. Whiskers. Front feet, pink, pushed out forwards, ready to spring back. For a little while we remained fixed, just so; and then there was a rustle higher up. I flicked my eyes up, briefly; and in that instant the woodmouse had darted away.

It went, I think, into a bramble bush a little way down; but I cannot be sure.

It did not rain.

It did not rain but that was fine.

It was all fine.

We walked well for five hours without stopping and covered a fair amount of ground, and as we went we saw the shape of a mountain appear at the horizon.

Mount Kulal.

Goat tracks in the sand, meanwhile.

A while later, two men in loincloths in the distance, carrying spears.

Further still and we came to a cluster of thorn trees, where goats and sheep were gathered in great numbers around a deep well, where seven men passed up water hand to hand in tin buckets, singing their water-song.

This place was called Intahe.

The Wells at Intahe

There was grazing for our camels to be had by the wells at Intahe, and the desert before had been lacking in it, and so, although it was only mid-afternoon, we made our camp there, while they ate their fill.

Our Rendille whiled away the time exchanging news with the men at the well, and with playing a game that involved a wooden board carved with two rows of cups, between which stones were moved.

The exchange of news took the form of extended monologues, with each man taking his turn to hold forth, while the others listened patiently for as long as the speaker cared to go on, while they marked the end of each of his sentences by exclaiming 'o-oh!' and 'e-eh!' alternately.

Frazer, Andy and I drank water, and splashed our hair and faces with it, and having some to spare, we also cleaned our teeth. And then we drank more water, cool and sweet from the well.

Then we spread out our sleeping-bags beneath a tree and lay back and watched the men talk and play their game.

A cow gave birth just in front of where we lay, and licked the mucus from her calf, and nudged the calf with her nose as it struggled to stand.

A while later, Osman took us to see a pile of earth, and beside it a deep hole, some sixty-five feet deep, by my reckoning. He said that a man had recently dug this in the hope of finding water, but without success.

How long it had taken him, I don't know.

But if the general pace of life we saw at Intahe was anything to go by, then quite some time, I reckon; what with all the talking and the playing of board-games and everything.

And I reckon that if you or I were to take it into our heads, where we live, to attempt something similar – I don't know, dig up the back garden looking for water or oil or buried treasure or something, armed with a rudimentary shovel and prepared to dig down as far as it takes for as long as it takes, then we'd probably need to make arrangements of some sort, to get it done. At the very least we'd need to take some time off work; get permission from the local authority planning department and Health and Safety people, all those sorts of things. Field the complaints from the neighbours, perhaps.

Whereas at Intahe – well, a man would just go out and dig: ten feet, twenty, thirty or more. And from time to time people might take a break from their herding or whatever to gather round and peer over the edge for a while, and stand and exchange views on the likelihood or otherwise of there being any water at the end of it all. And so it would go on.

I think, also, of how we came to be there in the first place. How we got our guides. How, on the very day of our arrival at Ilaut, Kibiriti had wandered into the Rendille encampment, and in a matter of minutes had managed to find two men who, at the drop of a hat, had agreed to spend a couple of weeks taking us 200-odd miles across the desert. Just like that.

It's how much time these people seem to have to do with as they please.

About a thousand hours a year is how much, to put a number on it.

It's been worked out.

Your typical pastoralist – your Samburu, your Rendille, your Turkana – he has a thousand hours more free time on his hands than you do, if you're in any way typical of the 'modern' world. And if you are in any way typical, then you will probably spend around 230 days a year in the office or the factory or wherever it is that you work. In which case a thousand extra free hours would work out for you at just over four hours a day to spend doing something else other than working. It would be like knocking off around lunchtime every day, rather than staying for the afternoon. And that would be every single working day for the whole of your life.

As for the pastoralists, so too for the hunter-gatherers: the Hiwi of South America spend an average of three hours a day doing what they have to do to get by. The Yanomami of the Amazon, meanwhile, get through their day's work in even less time: two hours and forty-eight minutes.

Our closest animal cousins, the apes and monkeys, they work just a touch harder: scientists say they spend around four and a half hours a day at the daily grind of eating fleas off each other and peeling bananas with their toes, or whatever else it is that counts for work in monkey-world. And then they're done.

If there is a 'natural' working day, a working day for which humankind evolved, then my bet is that these are all far closer to it than is the 'civilised' nine to five. Or even the 8:30 to 5:30, or the 8:30 to 6:00, or whatever it is that we all work these days. And not to mention the fact that the average 'lunch hour' in my part of the world now lasts twenty-two minutes, so they say, and consists, mostly, of a pre-packed supermarket sandwich in a card-board and cellophane box, consumed at one's desk while looking up stuff on the internet.

'Primitive affluence' is a phrase that's been used to describe what it is that people like the Rendille have.

Although the word 'primitive', these days, is considered a bit problematic, and something you're not really meant to say any more, because it might lead you to believe that living in a tiny mud-floored hut made of twigs plastered with animal-dung might be construed as being in some way 'primitive' in the sense of being less advanced or sophisticated than, say, living in a large brick-built house with electricity, hot and cold running water, electronically controlled gas-fired central heating and a big stainless-steel refrigerator in your kitchen with a special button on it that you can press to dispense ice-cubes of the size and consistency of your choosing directly into your glass.

Whereas . . . well, whatever.

But if we have these things, if we have televisions and microwave ovens, and if we have motor-cars and dishwashers and digital video-cameras and electric hair-straightening tongs, and if we have special mobile telephones that do more or less everything except make a cup of tea, then we pay for them.

We pay dearly for them with our lives and with our freedom.

And consequently we don't tend to spend what little time we have left to us digging bloody great holes in the ground in the off-chance that we might or might not find something of interest at the bottom of them.

Four Days at Gewani

They could go no further.

Without Miriam Muhammad, and with the soldiers refusing to proceed, there could be no question of moving further up country on the way to Aussa. Instead, they made camp on the plain near Gewani, Miriam Muhammad's home village, and there they stayed for four days and four nights.

During that time, there came into the camp a young chief by the name of Hamdo Ouga. Hamdo Ouga was a young man, about eighteen years old, and he was at this time rather pleased with himself, having recently overcome something of a shadow or a stain upon his reputation.

His father, a renowned warrior-chief, had died not long before, and Hamdo Ouga, being the eldest son, was, in theory, in line to succeed him. But to the discomfort of his entire village, he had only, in his entire life, killed one single man. This was considered really rather pitiful for someone wishing to call himself a chief. It would be like calling yourself an Aborigine, say, and being unable to get your boomerang to come back. There was, consequently, much talk in the shadows and much grumbling and muttering, and also much mention of other warriors with far more kills to their names who would, under the circumstances, make a far better and more credible job of the chieftaincy.

Realising the way the wind was blowing, Hamdo Ouga decided to make amends for his tardiness, and with a group of friends he set off into the lands of the Issa tribe on a 'big game hunting' expedition.

He returned a few days later with the severed genitalia of four men.

As for the manner in which these four men met their deaths, it was not recorded; though it is known that as a rule the Asaimara preferred to take their quarry unawares.

Whatever the method and whatever the circumstances, Hamdo Ouga's return was the occasion for much rejoicing, and his deeds were felt to have settled the matter of his fitness for the succession once and for all.

He came into Thesiger's camp fresh from the celebrations, all smiling and proud, his hair dressed with ghee and sporting both a feather plume and a wooden comb, and he had, besides, five leather thongs hanging from the sheath of his dagger.

Along with him came his companions, all grinning from ear to ear – some of those ears being newly split to mark their achievements. One or two warriors carried rather messy wounds from the large lead bullets of the nineteenth-century French *fusil gras* rifles carried by the Issa; but these wounds, apparently, were nothing to worry about, being surprisingly quick to heal, they said, in their considerable experience. Except when they killed you, of course – in which case they tended, as a rule, not to heal at all.

But whatever the wounds of his companions, the young man was jubilant.

'He struck me,' said Thesiger, 'as the Danakil equivalent of a nice, rather self-conscious Etonian who had just won his school colours for cricket.'

In the camp he was offered firm handshakes and hearty congratulations on his achievement, and everyone was happy.

Or rather, almost everyone was happy. The Issa, probably, were somewhat less than pleased about the whole affair, but their opinion didn't count for much among the Asaimara.

Four days later, however, Hamdo Ouga came up with the bright idea of trying his luck again, this time against the Adoimara further up the river on the way to Aussa – the way, in fact, that Thesiger's expedition would be heading if it ever got moving again. While he was at it, the young man hoped to recover from the Adoimara some cattle they had stolen.

They killed him, dead.

Then they took his accoutrements back with them to decorate their own trophy-cabinets.

Such was life, and such was death, among the tribes of those parts at that time.

'None of that worried me,' Thesiger was later to write. 'I'm not a missionary and I don't consider it's my duty to go round finding fault with other people's morals and behaviour. If they were living in Chelsea, I would say it was. I do have preferences but it's not my business to enforce those preferences on other people.'

And for all that, the Asaimara were, as he put it in his diary at the time, 'A cheerful, happy people despite the incessant killing, and certainly not afflicted by the boredom which weighs so heavily today on our own young urban civilisation.'

One of Hamdo Ouga's last acts had been to sell Thesiger an old and half-blind pony for fifteen dollars. A short while later it escaped and made its way back home, taking its new tack and saddle with it. It had, it turned out, done this on numerous occasions before, and, indeed, was notorious for it. But no one had thought it polite to mention the fact at the time.

The expedition, meanwhile, was going nowhere.

Miriam Muhammad might have been able to help, even if he could not himself have been persuaded to go to Aussa. However, he had been called away to sit in judgment over an unfortunate case in which a warrior had speared an old madwoman who had laughed constantly in the night and so disturbed his sleep. The warrior's defence was that it had all been a dreadful mistake: he had thought she was a hyena. A sort of two-legged, humanoid kind of hyena, dressed in human clothes, perhaps, and one looking suspiciously like an old madwoman. But it was dark, he said, and you can't always see what's what under such conditions. The woman's relatives, though, were having none of it and were crying out for blood. Or at least, if not blood, then substantial compensation in the form of goods and livestock.

Back in camp, meanwhile, one of the Somali camel-men had been looking at the .410 rifle Thesiger had given him, and had shot it off by mistake, nearly killing one of his companions, who had been lying in the tent next to him.

In the end, two things happened to break the deadlock.

The first was Thesiger's threat to remain exactly where he was for as long as it took, and to send all the soldiers back by train to explain why they had abandoned their mission.

The second was that Miriam Muhammad's nephew Ali agreed to take his uncle's place and to go with the expedition into Aussa, together with a chief called Ahmado to whom Thesiger took an instant dislike. Ali's presence, in particular, was sold to the soldiers as a major coup for the expedition and as the very next-best thing to having the Hangadaala himself with them: perhaps even better, since he was a fit young man who would not slow the expedition down in the way that his uncle would have.

It was thought prudent not to mention the fact that Ali had a number of enemies both further along the river and among his own people, who, rumour had it, considered him to be an arrogant loudmouth in need of taking down a peg or two.

Ahmado, as it turned out, also had a number of 'issues'. Particularly in relation to the people of Aussa. But these did not emerge until some time later.

Elsewhere

If you could look down on the world, and see everything that takes place upon the face of it, and if you were to pull your attention back from the small party camped by the course of the Awash River, further and further back, high above the tangle of trees at the water's edge and the desert land spreading wide on either side, and if you were to pull back high into the sky, and if you were then to look over to the west, across the land and across the deep and churning ocean beyond, and the boats like toys in the heaving swell, and if you were then to cast your eyes up to the north, to England, then as your glance passed upwards you would see, in time, a thin-soiled land of bare, broad hills, where sheep graze in stone-walled fields by thorn trees bent double by the wind. And in a wide valley in the midst of this land, you would see a great industrial town, with 360 huge brick-built cotton mills – one for each day of the year, more or less – and all working both day and night; and all surrounded by row upon row and street upon street of smoke-blackened slate-roofed red-brick terraces with drying washing hung upon the lines strung across the cobbled yards and alleys between them.

It is spring. It is morning. The sudden rain, having passed, has given way to blue skies and wisps of white cloud, though the

139

cobbles are still wet. And if you listen well, on this day, you will not hear the sound of machinery, as you might on any other day; and you will see, if you look closer, that the mills are still and shut; and you will see also that the streets of the town round about are not as you might expect them to be, and that the walls and the houses and the black iron lamp-posts are decked with boughs and flowers. Here, the white froth of blackthorn, there, the heavy scented hawthorn-blossom; and over the low house-doors you will see birch-branches wedged or fastened there, their rain-shower leaves trembling in the gentle breeze.

Though by the clock the working day has long since started, the streets are thronged with people; and by the gates of this mill here before you, a crowd of mill-girls has gathered, in their thin cotton frocks and their rough, home-knitted cardigans and their heavy lace-up clogs. And they have flowers in their hair: daisy-chains they wear.

And one of these girls is my grandmother.

And somewhere in the crowds is a little boy of three years old in hand-me-down shorts two sizes too big for him: my father.

And they have set up a maypole in the street, and set a sapling on top of it, and they have hung it about with boughs and garlands.

And there will be dancing in the streets of the town.

And, just for now, the machines will be silent and in their place the town will move to a different pace, and the rhythm of the seasons and the rhythm of the land and the rhythm of those long since dead will once more assert itself.

For the most part, though, life is the mill and the mill is life.

Ten-hour shifts, 300 days a year, each girl constantly pacing the floor between the machines, checking her assigned set of spindles for breaks in the thread, to be pieced together by twisting; for depleted bobbins of unspun cotton on the racks or creels, to be replaced; and for the build-up of loose cotton fibres on the machinery to be cleaned.

Three tasks, endlessly repeated for all your waking hours.

We are all on a journey here, you and I, and have been all down the generations. We've been on this journey ever since we put aside our feathers and our flint-tipped arrows and left our homes in the dappled shade of the forests to follow the grassland herds, or else to clear the land and till the fields; and we have been on this journey still in the years since we left those fields for the towns and the cities, and made our lives in the mills, like my grandmother, or in the factories, like my father, or in a suit and tie sorting cheques in the upstairs machine-room office of provincial high-street banks, like me. And where we are is where we are, and it's where we've ended up.

And most of the time we do not stop to calculate the profit and the loss, or to look back at the way we have come and ask ourselves whether that was the right way, or whether the distance has been too far or not far enough, or whether it is too late to go back and pick up some of the things we have lost or left behind along the way.

But it concerns us nevertheless.

Incidents on the Slopes of Mount Kulal

We set off early and walked without stopping for six hours, after which we reached the lower slopes of Mount Kulal.

We began to climb, and as we did so the ground became rocky, more thickly vegetated with dense dry grass, cactus and low thorn bushes. This bothered the camels, and they became fractious and picky about where they would place their feet, and they snorted and grumbled. At times they refused to move at all. It reached the point where we had to scout out the ground in front of them and guide their feet, in order to make any progress.

We climbed higher and higher, and as we climbed we could see before us spectacular views of a deep gorge in the mountain, and behind us spread out the vast expanse of the desert we had crossed thus far; and far in the distance, just on the horizon, we could see the blue silhouette of the hills by the wells at Ilaut, from which we had started.

It was hot again, despite the altitude, and the water we carried with us was, as ever, barely sufficient and carefully rationed out to make it last, but I had by now recovered fully from the effects of the heat of the early days. Acclimatisation, I suppose, was a big part of it. Also an old traveller's trick, which I shall share with you here and now, in case you should ever find yourself in a similar position to the one in which I found myself.

If you ever find yourself walking across a burning desert, oppressed by the heat of the sun to the extent that it makes you fall over and vomit, and then to behave like a complete and utter wet blanket for several days thereafter, then it may help you to look about your person or in your baggage for some form of headgear. You may, for example, have an Arab headscarf; or, if not, then you may have some piece of cloth or clothing with which you may fashion one for yourself.

If you do have such a thing about you, then what you should do with it is to put the bloody thing on your head.

You will be surprised at the difference it makes.

And you will be surprised also at your own stupidity for not having done it sooner.

I was congratulating myself for having worked this out, and feeling rather pleased about it, and also thinking, as we all did, about water and about ice-cold lemonade and about other things that we might drink, one day, when we got back, when, quite suddenly, something happened.

What happened was that I had diarrhoea.

By this, I don't mean that I felt a sudden need to go and squat down behind a bush, and then I had diarrhoea; or even that I pulled my shorts down and then did it.

What I mean is, *I had diarrhoea.*

This was unfortunate.

It was unfortunate for a number of reasons.

It was unfortunate because the only clothes I had with me were the ones that I was wearing. And also because the next water in which I might wash them was several days away.

Taking my shorts off and rubbing them in sand sort of cleaned them up a bit.

Luckily, they were brown anyway.

Looking back on it now, I could, I suppose, have used the drinking-water from my bottle. That would have cleaned them up a bit. Equally, I suppose, I could have cut off my own right arm, wrung it out and used the blood. However, neither alternative occurred to me at the time.

Lunch was *ugali*. We had run out of dried goat.

And here's a thing. Now, there may be some who like *ugali*. The Rendille, for example: they can't seem to get enough of it. But to me, boiled flour tastes rather like – well, boiled flour, actually. It may be marginally better than boiled sawdust, perhaps, but not by so much as you'd notice.

However, you would imagine that after however many days it is in the desert, and being beset by constant hunger and thirst and still visibly losing weight every day, then it might sort of taste better as you go on.

This was not the case, in my experience.

We pressed onto the top of the mountain, reaching it before nightfall, and there we came across a wide dirt track, which, Osman said, was the runway for the flying doctor. At the far end of this track we found an octagonal tin hut, beside which sat a man. The man greeted us and warned us to take care where we made our camp, because a lioness had lately taken to crossing in front of his hut at night, and heading off along a faint dirt track that he pointed out to us. Much better, he said, that we put our animals in the thorn-bush *kraal* on the far side, and make it firm and secure, and build up a big fire and sleep by that, taking turns to watch in the night.

This we did, and the night, or most of it, passed without event, almost until dawn.

My watch was a late one. After it I drew my sleeping-bag close to the fire and lay down, and listened out for lions for a while, until it struck me that I didn't really know what one would sound like, creeping up on you. It would be pretty quiet, I'd reckon, if not completely silent. And besides, Apa was squatting by the fire leaning on his spear, so I went to sleep instead.

I am a great enthusiast for sleeping.

I sleep soundly, most of the time, and I sleep long and well. It is a talent of mine, sleeping, and a great pleasure to me also. It is something that I have perfected over many years of diligent practice.

I have done this on the floors of coaches and trains, on the decks of boats being lashed by spray, and once, dressed in a business-suit and with a briefcase as my pillow, on the marble floor of Barcelona airport, having got up and arrived at some unearthly hour of the morning only to find that I had turned up at the wrong terminal. By the time I discovered this, my plane was leaving from the terminal I should have been at, and as a consequence I had to wait for the next plane, which was some four hours later; and so I lay down there and slept. The sleep was delicious, despite all of the people walking by; and it was made all the more so by the knowledge that I had set the alarm on my mobile phone to wake me up in just enough time to buy a pastry and a strong *cortado* coffee before boarding my flight.

But when the screaming started I was up and out of my sleeping-bag in an instant. As were we all.

It was the camels. The camels were screaming, if you can imagine such a thing; and as they screamed they reared and charged at their thorn-bush wall, in a frantic attempt to break through; and the two Rendille were running around to the far side with their spears and sticks, and Andy was upending the sack in which the pangas were kept and Frazer grabbed two and passed me one and we ran around.

And then nothing.

Rock and scrub beneath a starry sky.

Rock and scrub and stars and the shadows of the night, and the earth spinning silently on its axis in the endless depths of space.

I don't know, sometimes. I just don't know.

Upon Sleep, Pleasure and Duty

The longer I live, these days, the less I seem to understand about people, and how life works.

I mentioned sleep, a while back. I do know that many people take a different view of it to the one I take. Which is fine.

Some people, upon waking up in bed early on a Sunday morning, would not lay there for several hours more, luxuriating in the wonderfulness of it, but rather would get up and go and do something useful instead.

Some people take great pride in how little sleep they can get away with, and how constantly busy they are. Politicians, for example, and captains of industry.

But here's the thing: I had assumed that it was their pleasure so to do, just as it was my pleasure to do otherwise; and that the driving force in all human life, beyond the mere necessity of things, was pleasure.

Or, better still, that living, as distinct from merely being alive, was the art of making pleasure out of necessity.

We have to eat. We have to sleep. We have to make our way in the world. There is any number of things that we have to do to get by and to get on.

So we might as well enjoy them, or else what would be the point?

Aristotle says something similar in his *Nicomachean Ethics*. What he says, in essence, is that pleasure is the completion or perfection of human life. That even though the things that bring pleasure may vary dramatically from person to person, yet in its essence all pleasure is one and the same thing, and is distinct from mere transient 'fun' or distraction, which often ends up in a far greater quantity of misery or dissatisfaction. For Aristotle, pleasure is the attainment of serious, deep-seated and long-lasting happiness.

Suffering spontaneous diarrhoea in your shorts may not strike you as a particularly pleasurable sort of thing to do, but I would not have had it otherwise. Well, not now, anyway. At the time it was a bit of a surprise, and not, I'd say, altogether fun.

But I felt then, and feel still, that I was living, rather than just being alive.

And I feel, now, joy and gratitude in being able to write about it, and to be able to say, I did this.

But there are people who seem to go out of their way not to have pleasure, or who seem to think that pleasure is somehow frivolous or unworthy while there are more important things to be done.

I read a while ago about a man, an American man, who built up a business in his twenties and then sold it for one and a half billion dollars. Ten years on, he's working twelve-hour days in an office. At least. Gets in at eight, works till eight, nine, ten. And his wife has a job, too.

Which would be all well and good if that was what gave them pleasure, and yet between them, they say, they struggle to find the time to be together, and this causes them concern.

'My wife has a stressful job,' he says. 'She works in the financial services sector.'

She has a job in the financial services sector.

She has one and a half billion dollars to her name.

In what way, stressful?

In what conceivable universe could she feel anything even remotely resembling 'stress' about her job performance, or concern about the fate of other people's money, when she has so much of it herself?

So she fails. So they sack her. And then what?

For what reason could either of them, the husband or the wife, not be able to find the time to do what they want to do?

Is this living? Or is it merely being alive?

And I read also a newspaper interview with a pair of athletes, a brother and a sister, who both trained furiously at the triathlon, and who achieved a considerable degree of success at it. They both did this training, running, swimming and cycling, for many, many hours a day, day in and day out. Which, in itself, is no bad thing. I know people who love doing triathlons, even though I've never been tempted myself.

If you have things that you love to do, and if you love to do them more than almost anything else in life, then to be able to devote most of your waking hours to doing them well would seem to be the perfect pleasure.

Except that in this interview, both the brother and the sister said that neither of them actually enjoyed the cycling.

Or the running.

Or, indeed, the swimming.

Which, when you put them all together, *is* the triathlon.

'I was never going to be a swimmer,' said the brother, in his interview. 'I wasn't big enough and I never really enjoyed it. I still don't enjoy it now. To be honest, most of the time I don't like swimming, cycling *or* running.'

Despite which, he spends thirty hours a week doing them.
And about which he says:

'There really isn't a whole lot of excitement with training thirty hours a week. It's a nightmare. Most of the time you're very tired, and the tiredness accumulates . . . it catches up with you and you get this massive low . . . I don't feel I'd be where I am today without complete self-sacrifice.'

Complete self-sacrifice. And for what, exactly?

It wasn't just him, either. The whole family seemed to be like it. Here is the sister:

'We trained at different times at different pools when we were kids, so my mum used to spend half her life driving us back and forth . . . I don't think we showed any particular talent at that age, but Mum just didn't like us quitting things.'

Mum just didn't like us quitting things – I have read that sentence over and again since first coming across the article, and I cannot but think of what a joyless, miserable, utterly pleasureless existence these people must have.

It shakes my understanding of human nature, that there should be people who live in this way.

Bicycle thieves I can understand, even though I might want to beat them to a pulp. And also those people who gain their pride and pleasure and status from killing, who split their ears in celebration of it and who adorn themselves with the marks and badges of their murderous ways – even at the risk of being themselves killed. I can see how they fit into the world, even though I wouldn't want to find myself on the wrong side of them. There is a heady potency to them, a power and a swagger; and so long as they confine themselves to killing each other – or maybe the occasional outsider who enters their land in full knowledge of the risks – then I can't see how it's anyone's business to stop them.

But these relentless, sensible, duty-driven people, they unsettle me.

Into Hostile Territory

The expedition headed north for nine days, and a hard going they had of it. The land by the river's edge was difficult, and at times was thickly forested. To make matters worse, they were obliged to stop at every village they passed, to receive from the headmen gifts of sheep – to the point where they were driving along with them a substantial flock, which grew faster than it could be eaten. They were also required to preside at dances held in their honour. In return for these things there was an expectation that they would donate to the village items from their own supplies, and each of the men found themselves constantly beset by outstretched palms on all sides, and requests for ammunition, for spare belts and shoes, for pots and pans and even for the very clothes they wore.

But move they did, though painfully slowly, and by the end of the second day they found themselves at a large open plain, enclosed on three sides by forest, and on the fourth side, slanting away before them, they saw a range of extraordinarily coloured hills, streaked and variegated in every shade: mauve, orange, brick-red, yellow and white.

These, said the Asaimara guides, were the Asdar Hills. They marked the frontier between Bahdu and a land called Borhamala, in which lived many bands of Adoimara. Some of whom, no doubt, were at that very time sitting by their huts gazing proudly at the pole upon which they had hung the various body-parts of Hamdo Ouga, while lazily picking from their teeth the last fragments of the cattle that he had set out to recover from them.

They moved onward with apprehension, noting the numerous Adoimara villages upon the slopes of the hills, and also the large numbers of fortified kraals and defiles round about, the evidence of much raiding and retaliation.

But the tribes kept away.

Or at least, they mostly kept away.

One day, however, Thesiger's party set up camp, only to notice a short while later that they had one less camel than when they had stopped. They looked round about but it was nowhere to be seen. The Somali camel-men set off further up river to look for it, and some two miles from camp they spotted two armed Adoimara driving it away.

When the camel-men opened fire on them the warriors bolted and the camel was recovered, but it was a sign that there was a need for constant vigilance. The next raiding-party could be bigger – considerably bigger, given the number of villages in the vicinity.

The military escort, meanwhile, was in the process of falling apart.

They had always been unwilling participants in the expedition. Their levels of readiness were never high, not even at the best of times; but by now whatever discipline or cohesion they had ever had crumbled and their headman lost all semblance of control over them. They were, mostly, unwilling now to do any work or even to stand sentry-duty. Instead, they spent their time bickering and squabbling among themselves.

In an effort to ease their passage through the land of the Adoimara and to head off the possibility of an attack that they were ill-equipped and ill-prepared to defend themselves from, Ali went out with a party to the nearest village and sought out the elders, telling them that they came with an Englishman who was a great doctor, and who, if they gave him safe passage through their land, would heal their sick and injured with the medical supplies he carried with him.

The offer was accepted, and messengers were sent out to pass the word around the surrounding villages.

Within a short while, a great number of men, women and children had made their way to the camp shivering with fever, groping their way blindly with badly infected eyes – to which they seemed, as a race, to be unusually prone – and also carrying on their bodies a suppurating fungus-like growth, which ate away great chunks of flesh, and which, if it healed, left the most appalling scars. And in addition there were any number of gougings, gashings, woundings and manglings from spear and *fusil gras*.

Thesiger had had experience of doctoring in Bahdu, and, by and large, the Asaimara had been pleased with the results. So it was with the Adoimara of Borhamala.

Again Thesiger's party moved on up the river, painfully slowly, in short marches followed by endless halts for more doctoring – for word had spread far faster and further than they had anticipated – until they left the villages behind and came, at last, to a series of deep and rocky ravines which they could not cross.

The only alternative open to them was to follow the ravines around, even though they stretched for many miles on either side. This they did, and it took them far out into the stony desert to the east known as Adou or 'the place of thirst'.

They rejoined the Awash five days later at a place called Abakaboro, where there were fresh-water wells ten feet deep, and they made their camp beneath umbrella-thorn trees on the bank nearby.

A little way from where they rested they could see the remains of some fortifications. These had been built some four years before by a large band belonging to the Wagerat tribe. They had been destroyed shortly afterwards when the Wagerat were confronted by a force sent against them by the Sultan of Aussa.

The Sultan did not take kindly to outsiders straying into his lands.

On the horizon, across the river and beyond the ruined fortifications, they could now see the Magenta Mountains, the border of his kingdom.

That day, Thesiger sent Ali and two companions ahead on a mission.

It was one on which not only the success or failure of the expedition depended, but their lives also.

They were to make contact with the Sultan.

The original plan had been for Ali to take with him Ahmado, his companion from Miriam Muhammad's village, but at this point a slight difficulty emerged. Ahmado, who had been chosen to accompany the expedition to Aussa, actually came from a family that had a long-standing and vicious blood-feud with the people of Aussa. And also, as it happened, with many of the people in the villages surrounding their current camp. God knows why he was sent: perhaps this kind of thing was what counted for humour among the Asaimara, and perhaps his kinsmen were even at that moment rolling on the ground outside their huts clutching their sides with mirth.

The three men left, and those who remained waited and hoped.

Night fell, and mosquitoes swarmed from the river in vast numbers and sucked their blood. The next day came and went, and the mosquitoes came again; and the same the next, and the next, and all that they could do was to wait and hope.

From time to time local Adoimara warriors came to their camp, with messages for Ahmado. Once they said that their people had prepared a feast for him, and would he like to go along? He would not, as it happened.

On another occasion they said that they had some Asaimara women in their village who were keen to meet him; but on this occasion and on every other one – and there were many – when they came for him, Ahmado refused to move away from the door of Omar's tent.

On the seventh day, Thesiger went out to shoot some game.

He returned to find that three strange warriors had been in camp, asking many questions about their purpose and their destination and the nature of the things they carried with them. In particular, they had been especially keen to know whether the expedition had a machine gun.

Omar thought they had been sent by the Sultan.

This could be a good sign, he said.

Or else it could be a very bad one.

The next day Ali returned, bringing the news.

He had been away for eight days.

Telling the Sheep from the Goats

We descended on the farther side of Mount Kulal, which was steeper than the side that we had climbed: steeper and rockier, and the camels were unhappy about it, and did not hesitate to let us know. We were obliged, again, to guide their feet, which was hot work, hot and dry.

There had been cool cloud about us when we set off, but as the morning wore on we left it far behind us, or it burnt off, or both; and the sun beat down on us more fiercely than at any time on our journey so far. It promised to become hotter still, where we were going, for spread out far below us we could see the shimmering heat of a wide plain strewn as far as the eye could see with a lifeless rubble of black volcanic rocks.

By midday we had managed to get the camels about halfway down the mountain, and we stopped in what little shadow was afforded by a large rock to make lunch, which was, as ever, boiled *ugali*.

As we sat, a speck appeared in the desert below us. It was moving towards us, growing larger as it approached. As it climbed up towards our camp, we recognised it at last as a *moran*. He greeted us when he reached us, and we him, and then he sat with us and exchanged news with our camel-men, according to the custom of his people. This took some time, but no one was in any hurry, it seemed; and at some point in the conversation Osman turned towards us and said that the *moran* was, in fact, a nephew of Apa. He seemed to have rather a lot of cousins and nephews.

And then, quite suddenly, the *moran* stood up, and turned around and made his way back down the mountain. We watched him go, and as he went he planted his spear in the ground to steady himself against the slope, and gradually he became smaller and smaller until he appeared to be no more than a tiny speck on the plain. We looked at Osman – he sat, clutching his knees, smiling to himself as if somewhat deep in thought. The two Rendille were similarly disposed.

Frazer opened his mouth to speak, as if he were about to say, 'Shall we pack up?' but Osman raised his hand as if to say, 'Not now – all will become clear soon.'

And, indeed, it did, in time. Rather a lot of time, as it happens, but it did become clear in the end as we saw the speck on the plain again, coming towards us once more. He was walking rather strangely this time, and appeared to be hunched or carrying a burden of some kind across his shoulders. He was. For as he climbed the rocky slope we could make out, eventually, the shape of the goat carcass that he carried.

Reaching where we sat, he flung down the goat and grinned, at us all, and said something in his language which I imagine would have translated as,

'What do you want to eat that *ugali* rubbish for when I've brought you some proper food, eh?'

He and our Rendille between them cooked some of the meat on our fire, and the remainder of the skinned carcass they split down the middle along the backbone, as butchers do. One half was put into a sack and loaded up onto one of our camels;

the other half the *moran* hefted back up onto his shoulder and, with a cheery goodbye wave, set back off down the mountain.

We reached the plain in the mid-afternoon. It was hot such as I have never known, and yet the going was easier than it had been on the mountainside in spite of it, and the camels more willing.

Towards nightfall we reached some hills where it seemed that there might be water, or at least grazing, for we began to encounter flocks of what I would have described as goats, but which were, apparently, sheep.

'When the Son of Man shall come in His glory,' the Bible says, 'and all the holy angels with Him, then shall he sit upon the throne of His glory. And before Him shall be gathered all nations: and He shall separate them one from another, as a shepherd divideth his sheep from the goats.'

I'd never considered that too much of a challenge, to tell the truth. It had always struck me as the sort of task that even I could manage, if He had happened to be indisposed, for some reason, on the Day of Judgment. And I've never done any shepherding in my life. Big white woolly things shaped like clouds but with dirty backsides – those are your sheep; and your goats are the others, the narrow-faced short-haired ones with the sticky-up horns who try to eat everything.

Bloody townies, eh?

But in that part of the world the sheep and the goats look remarkably similar, to the point of being practically identical, and telling the one from the other was considerably trickier – apart from the sheep, from the back, having slightly fatter, more blubbery tails. But what if you had a scrawny sheep? Or what if you had a goat with a fat backside? Would they still be sheep and goat respectively? Or would they, in fact, become goat and sheep? And how would you know?

It makes one wonder whether there might be countries in the world where other things we think of as being very different are, in fact, considerably less so: wheat and chaff, for example; or men and boys. Or whether there might, somewhere, even, be a nation whose inhabitants genuinely do find it difficult to distinguish between their arses and their elbows.

Maybe in the kingdom of the blind, where the one-eyed man is king.

We made our camp beneath a tree in the shadow of a cliff, on top of which a troop of baboons played lazily, and there we lit our fire. Presently we were joined at it by a pair of Turkana, who sat with us long into the night.

We sat, then, on our outspread sleeping-bags; and when, at last, I came to get into mine I found, to my surprise, that it was already taken, for there was in it a great spider of the most extraordinary proportions, the like of which I have never seen – not even in the zoo, and not even in pet-shops, and I've been to a few of those in my time – and which, were it not for its eight legs, it might easily have been mistaken for a small sheep. Or indeed goat.

The Silver Baton of Command

The Sultan, said Ali, was courteous. Courteous but deeply suspicious.

The conversation had lasted for the greater part of an entire day. The Sultan had wanted to know, in detail, why were they approaching the borders of his land, and where they intended to go, and for what purpose, precisely, they were following the river. He listened politely to Ali's replies, taking small sips, from time to time, from the cup proffered to him by the waiting slave, and then asked the same questions all over again, in a slightly different form, and listened again to the answers, before suggesting in the end that the party might prefer, instead, to take the route around Aussa, for which he would provide them with an escort.

Ali bowed, and then replied that the Englishman, unfortunately, was determined to proceed in the direction he had chosen.

To which the Sultan folded his hands across his stomach and replied that in which case the Englishman should do so, then. And in the meantime he would decide what action to take, or not take, at his leisure.

And now, his guests might wish to return to their camp to inform the Englishman of his words.

Ali's small group had not travelled far from the borders of Aussa when they met a large party of Danakil who, seeing their appearance and the direction from which they had come, assumed them to be the Sultan's men.

They hailed Ali, and warned him to be on his guard and to watch out for a band led by an accursed *Ferenghi*, Foreigner, down by the river. This *Ferenghi*, they said, had a machine gun and many rifles, and although he had not yet hurt anyone, was probably waiting his moment to raid their lands. But unbeknown to him, he was being watched from afar by three separate war-parties who had been following his progress.

And, they said, before bidding goodbye, Ali should also be aware of a second band of outsiders on the river, a large and well-armed group from the Wagerat tribe, one day's march away, who had raided Adoimara lands and stolen many cattle.

Ali thanked them for their information and hurried off to tell Thesiger the news.

'Well,' he said, when they told him, 'we must press on, then.'

Two days later, as the expedition was setting up camp, two elderly *askaris* or officers of the Sultan arrived, one of them holding in his hand a stout bamboo stick bound about with bands of engraved silver. They said that they had come far and fast and were weary, and they pressed the expedition to stop and set up camp nearby.

Ali and his companions fell back before the visitors, and immediately began doing their bidding. Thesiger, sensing their importance, led them to a place of honour and had food and drink brought for them from their supplies, which were, at this stage, rapidly depleting: even their once-large flock of sheep was now all eaten.

The *askaris* spoke to the Englishman through Ali, asking his business once more and repeating the Sultan's suggestion that the party take the shortest route to the French Somaliland border, rather than following the river through the heart of Aussa.

Thesiger thanked them for their interest in his plans, but informed them that it was their intention to move forward towards Aussa, if the Sultan would be so gracious as to allow them to pass.

'In which case,' said the senior *askari*, 'we shall see what the Sultan has in mind for you. But for now your people need better food.'

And with this he and his companion set off in the direction of the nearest village.

While he was gone, Ali explained that the stick the head *askari* carried was the silver baton of command, which gave the bearer the authority of the Sultan himself, and that no Danakil in or around Aussa, on pain of a crippling fine or worse, may refuse any request made by the bearer of the baton.

Sure enough, the *askaris* soon returned, bringing with them sheep and goats they had requisitioned from the elders of the village, which were then slaughtered and cooked.

Playing British Bulldog for a Bride

In the morning the baboons had gone.

We packed up our camels and set off, soon leaving the shelter of the hills behind and heading out once more across a flat desert plain strewn with black volcanic rocks. On the far side, towards the horizon, we could see a shimmering expanse that appeared, at first, to be a trick of the light, but which remained, no matter how we looked at it, and which, as the day wore on, became clearer and clearer as a vast expanse of water, in the middle of the dry and empty land.

'That,' said Osman, 'is Lake Turkana.'

It was a remarkable sight: so much water – so much.

We made our way across the plain towards a point on the lake's shore, a settlement called Loyangalani, where, beside a stand of tall palm trees, we could see a great many huts of different styles and shapes. We walked purposefully and fast, drawn by the lure of water, and eventually reached the place around lunchtime, coming first, at its edge, to a metal pipe set in a concrete base, from which gushed pure, clear water the temperature of a warm bath, from which we drank until we were fit to burst, and with which I was able, at last, to wash my shorts.

The huts in Loyangalani were of all of the tribes and cultures in the area, the most common being igloo-shaped Turkana huts made of straw matting and bound bundles of dry palm-leaves, but there were also thatched wattle-and-daub huts built around frames of wooden branches, as well as a number of small houses made of whitewashed stone with sloping tin roofs. Beyond these, we could see the larger shapes of a mission church and a school.

After drinking from the pipe we went to an eating-house owned by yet another of Apa's relatives – his sister, this time – and there we had sweet tea made with ginger and bread made in a frying-pan. Pan-fried bread is something the Sioux Indians make, also, preparing a dough with flour, water and baking-powder and frying it on both sides in a hot pan. In that place, at that time, it tasted unimaginably wonderful.

Finally, Apa's sister brought us cups of water which was cool, and which was beyond words to describe.

This water was made cool in a most miraculous way – which, apparently, is quite simple science, and the same process by which sweating cools you down or by which waterskins keep liquids from becoming too warm, but which, when you see it, still seems counterintuitive and magical.

What they do is they take a water-container – in this case, one of our jerry-cans – and they fill it with water and tie it inside a wet sack. Then they hang it in the hottest place they can find – in a tree in full sunlight, say – and then, when the sack is dry they pour out the water and it is cold, as if it had come from a refrigerator.

After this, Frazer, Andy and I walked to the lake with two little Turkana boys we met, and went swimming in the water there. Though we could not speak to each other, the language of jumping and splashing is a universal one, as is laughter.

I think that if there were to be a heaven, then it would feel something like this.

I do not know how long we were there for.

When we emerged, at last, a hot, dry wind had got up, and in places it swirled and twisted, calling up 'dust-devils' some twenty feet high on the plain.

Going back up to our camp we passed a group of fishermen from the Elmolo tribe on their way back home with their catch, and we bought two large Nile perch from them, to have that night as a change from goat.

We all spent most of the rest of the day resting, and trying – and failing – to get out of the oppressive heat of the burning wind, and also talking to our companions about our lives, and where we had come from. The two Rendille camel-men were particularly keen to learn about marriage customs in England, and were amazed to hear, as Osman translated our words for them, that we could have only one wife where we came from. This amazement turned to frank disbelief when the matter of bride-price arose.

'So you are telling me,' said Apa, 'that in your country the father of a girl will just *give* her away?'

'That's right.'

'For nothing?'

'And to a stranger he hardly knows?'

'It does happen.'

The two Rendille exchanged looks.

'It is impossible!'

We assured them that it wasn't, and that this really was the case, but they didn't look convinced. I think they thought we were making a joke at their expense.

Wedding customs that seem perfectly normal in your own country often seem downright odd to people from other places. But they often say a lot about your nation.

The Danakil of the lands around Aussa had a set of customs governing marriage that would probably seem very queer indeed to more or less anyone else. Being the kind of people that they were, these customs tended to revolve around various forms of ritual violence.

Among the Asaimara band, a man was expected to win his bride by organising a game rather like the one that small boys in England know as British Bulldog.

A young man wishing to marry would be expected to gather together eight of his friends and go to the house of the girl to ask her father for her hand in marriage. If the father agreed, then the girl would go out and gather together a similar number of her girlfriends and line them up some 200 or 300 yards from her house. Then the man would get his friends to line up halfway between them and the house – all apart from one, a man chosen by the groom, who, together with the girl, would stand by the house itself. Then the groom and the bride's father would retire to the sidelines and a signal would be given, upon which the girl would set off at a run, with the 'best man' in pursuit, aiming to dodge or break through the line of men to reach her girlfriends on the other side. If she managed to do so without being caught, then the wedding was off and the man had to try again a year later. If, however, she was caught, she was carried to her father's house and thrown roughly on the ground before it, and the wedding could take place. After the wedding, the couple was expected to live in the girl's village for a year, following which the man could take her back to his own village.

Among the Adoimara band, a man wishing to marry had to visit the girl's father on an allotted day and pay him three dollars, upon which he would be told that the girl was out grazing goats in such-and-such a place, and that he had leave to go and take her. The girl, meanwhile, would have chosen a high place with a good lookout to graze her goats, and would have with her an escort of girlfriends. Between them they would have collected a substantial arsenal of rocks, stones and sticks, and when they saw the man approaching they would attempt to drive him off, throwing the rocks and stones and beating him with the sticks. Depending on the willingness of the girl to marry the particular suitor, he could find the resistance rather easy to overcome, or else he could be seriously injured. This was frequently the case, apparently. On occasion men were even killed.

If captured, the girl would be taken back to her father, who would order the man to go away and come back with a he-camel. The girl, dressed in her finest clothes, would be tied to the camel's back and led three times around her father's house, watched by the entire village, while the beast, which would be very wild, bucked and kicked, and generally shook the girl all over the place. This done, the girl was lifted down and laid upon one of the best sleeping mats, and then swung backwards and forwards by four singing women.

Wedding customs change. Where I come from, weddings mostly took place in the bride's parish church, and at the culmination of the ceremony the groom would place a gold ring upon her finger. Increasingly, these days, there is a second gold ring involved, which the bride then places on the groom's finger. People still do get married in the bride's parish church, but a lot of people now get married elsewhere. It is becoming more common for a couple to go to another country, and to get married there in a ceremony of their choice or devising, and often in strange or unusual circumstances. They may, for example, get married in a chapel in Las Vegas by a man dressed in imitation of Elvis Presley; or on a beach, or parachuting from an aeroplane, or under the sea wearing aqualungs.

It has also become possible, in my country, for a man to marry another man and for a woman to marry another woman; or at least, for them to go through a ceremony which is a marriage in all but name. It is not permitted, however, for a man to marry his dog, or for his dog to marry his cat or anything of that kind, athough in some other countries where same-sex weddings between humans are unheard of, marriages between humans and animals and between animals and animals are nevertheless not unknown.

Children in parts of rural India are sometimes married off to animals, to protect them from the attentions of evil spirits. And I read recently about a case in the Sudan where a man married a goat. Marriage was not his original intention, apparently. However, one night, in a drunken state, he took advantage of the animal, perhaps having mistaken her for a sheep. He was not quiet about it; and hearing the noises of it, the enraged owner came out of his house and caught him at it, and pinned him down and tied him up, and hauled him next day before a council of tribal elders, who sat in judgment upon him and announced that he should do the decent thing by the goat, all things considered; and that he should also pay the owner a dowry of 15,000 dinars into the bargain.

They were pronounced man and goat shortly afterwards.

The former owner, interviewed by a newspaper some months later, said 'As far as I know they are still together.'

Sometimes in new kinds of marriage, remnants of ancient and long-dead customs may be found, such as in the use of decorated wooden spoons or old shoes as wedding-gifts or as adornments for the wedding-car or carriage after the ceremony. These were once given by the family of the bride to the groom, as representations of the father's authority to discipline his daughter and its handing-over over to her new husband.

There are customs also concerning childbirth, as for all significant milestones in life and in death, and these change also. There is, for example, now a custom in which, when a woman gives birth, her husband – or the man known as her *partner* if they are unmarried – stands in the hospital delivery-room dressed in a surgical gown and watches the proceedings. In many cases he will record the event with a video-camera.

The orthodoxy of one's own time and place, and the customs and rituals that go with it, always tend to seem much more natural and sensible than those of others. It takes, sometimes, something of a mental shift to see them otherwise.

In 1956, an anthropologist called Horace Miner wrote and published a paper called 'Body Ritual among the Nacirema', about the strange ways of a little-known tribe living in North America, in a territory between the Canadian Cree, the Yaqui and Tarahumare of Mexico, and the Carib and Arawak of the Antilles. Among these people, he said, there was a powerful belief that the human body is ugly and that its natural tendency is to debility and disease; and that consequently they must devote themselves to frequent ritual and ceremonial purifications, carried out in private and in secret in special household shrines devoted to the purpose. Such was the importance of these rituals to the Nacirema that the powerful and important individuals would often possess several such shrines, and the opulence of a house would often be referred to in terms of the number of them that it possessed. Inside, each shrine would contain a box or chest built into the wall, inside which there would be many charms and magical potions obtained from medicine men and herbalists, and without which the natives believed they could not live. Beneath the charm-box there would be a small font, and each day every member of the family, in succession, would enter the shrine room, bow his head before the charm-box, mingle different sorts of holy water in the font, and proceed with a rite of ablution.

The joke being, of course, that 'Nacirema' is American spelt backwards, and what Miner was describing was the obsessive cleanliness of his own people.

That evening we ate fish.

I say we ate fish, but by this I mean that Frazer, Andy, the two Samburu from Maralal and I ate it. The Rendille, on the other hand, did not. Not only did they not eat it but they were horrified and revolted at the very idea of it. They would not touch it, nor even anything that it had touched, and they insisted that the pot used to cook it in and the plates used to eat it from should be kept separate from then onwards.

Because they would not eat it, we had more than we needed for that day and so we only cooked one of the two fish, which we ate while the Rendille sat tucking into their goat and *ugali* and looking at us in disbelief.

The other fish we cleaned that night and decided to keep for the next evening. We considered different ways of storing it, and in the end went for Andy's suggestion of putting it in a plastic carrier-bag, and hanging it in the branches of a tree.

'It'll keep the insects off,' he said.

The Sultan's Vizier

Thesiger's expedition pressed on for five days after the meeting with the *askaris*, passing through increasingly rocky and desolate country, between two chains of hills, along the sides of which many strong fortifications had been built. On the fifth day they left the hills behind them and crossed a vast open plain, on the far side of which was a ridge of black rock, beyond which there was grazing for the camels, where they made their camp, although it was yet only mid-afternoon.

They had not been there for long when they saw a party of warriors, some thirty strong, advancing towards them from a distance. The warriors were all clad in spotless white loincloths and *shammas*, or togas, and all carrying rifles, and at their head rode a white-clad elder on a mule, while boys followed behind, driving a number of animals.

This was clearly an important party, and Thesiger quickly chivvied his soldiers to smarten up and look alert. They, also, sensing the importance of the imminent arrivals, put on a good show of it, so that in a matter of moments they had formed a guard of honour, ready to receive whoever might arrive.

They visitors halted at the edge of the camp, and two men stepped forward and helped the elder down from his mule. The warriors' front teeth, Thesiger noticed, were all filed down into points.

The elder, it transpired, was the Sultan's vizier, Kenyazmatch Yaio, the second-most important man in Aussa.

Thesiger greeted him with tea, and the vizier responded by signalling to the boys, who led out three magnificent bulls and six sheep.

'A gift from my master, the Sultan,' he said.

Thesiger and Ali inspected the beasts and commented on how fine they were, and thanked the vizier profusely; and he, having taken his tea and accepted their gratitude, informed them that the Sultan would shortly make his will known, and then departed with his retinue to a nearby village to spend the night.

That night, for some reason, the camp was surrounded by large numbers of hyenas, which howled and cackled without cease.

Some among the party considered it to be an omen.

A Magnificent Bearded Loon

That there should be sultans in the world; that there should be viziers and silver batons of command; that there should be Hangadaalas and men destined from birth to be the hereditary bearers of the various specified legs of Hangadaalas' chairs: these things say something about human nature, I think. And also that there should be people in the world who think it all so much stuff and nonsense and wish it all swept away.

You're either on one side or t'other here, I find, and the side you're on says much about the sort of person that you are, in all sorts of ways.

In the country where I come from there was a big to-do, a while back, about the House of Lords.

The government of the day was one that liked to think of itself as a rather modern, progressive sort of government, composed of the sorts of people who, if they'd ever had a silver baton of command, wouldn't have, because they'd have done away with it. They'd have melted it down, or else sold it off and used the money for some worthy project or other, with the aim of reducing social exclusion, in a very real sense, among the socially excluded, or some such stuff.

At this time, Britain was alone in the industrialised world in having one of its two Houses of Parliament composed largely of hereditary noblemen and noblewomen.

This wasn't thought to be a very modern or progressive thing at all.

Consequently, it was decided to turf as many of them out as was possible. Originally it was going to be the whole lot, but to smooth the process of the bill through Parliament it was proposed, in the end, that 700 of them should go, while the remaining ninety-two would be allowed to stay on for the time being.

This was agreed by the House of Commons.

But for the bill to become law, it also had to be agreed by the Lords themselves; many of whom, as you can imagine, were rather less than thrilled at the prospect.

Nevertheless, by a combination of political pressure and an alliance of appointed, or 'life', peers, the government managed to get the bill into a position where it was sure to be passed.

This was in 1999; and at the time of the vote, which took place in the October of that year, the chamber of the Lords was packed, both by the peers themselves and also by their eldest sons, who, as tradition dictated, were allowed to sit at the edge of the chamber on the steps to the throne, though not, under any circumstances, to take part in the debate. Passions, however, were running high.

So it happened that in the middle of the debate, and before the vote, one of these eldest sons stepped forward.

He was a striking figure, a magnificent bearded loon by the name of Charles Francis Topham de Vere Beauclerk, Earl of Burford and heir apparent to the Duke of St Albans, the Hereditary Grand Falconer of all England. Hitherto, Burford had been known only as the vigorous sponsor of the somewhat unconventional theory that the works of William Shakespeare were not, in fact, written by William Shakespeare, but by his own ancestor, Edward de Vere, 17th Earl of Oxford. You might have thought that the name 'William Shakespeare' printed on the title-pages of the plays and poems might have given a sharp-eyed literary scholar a bit of a clue to the author's identity, but that's all by the bye here, for this Earl of Burford rushed out onto the floor of the chamber, forcing the Lords' Deputy Speaker, Lord Boston of Faversham, to jump out of his way, and he climbed up onto the Woolsack, which is a large red cushion on the floor of the house that symbolises the source of England's wealth in the Middle Ages.

'My lords!' he shouted, waving his order-paper. 'This bill, drafted in Brussels, is treason!'

The Serjeant at Arms, General Sir Edward Jones, also known as Black Rod, moved to pull Burford down, but he resisted and continued to yell.

'What we are witnessing,' he shouted, 'is the abolition of Britain! Before us lies the wasteland, no Queen, no culture, no sovereignty, no freedom. Stand up for your Queen and country – vote this treason down.'

It was, it must be said, faintly ridiculous.

Some might say that it was more than faintly so: that it was wholly and utterly ridiculous. The newspapers certainly seemed to think it so.

And yet it was, at the exact same time, desperately sad.

A Fish Supper

We spent the whole of the next day in Loyangalani while the camels were thoroughly fed and watered.

We swam again, and explored the small grove of palm-trees by the town. It had a distinctive smell, this grove. This was because there was, in the midst of the trees, a clearing, and in this clearing the ground was dotted with the results of people using the place as a public lavatory.

We found a milestone on the edge of the dirt track leading off down the lakeside; it said 'South Horr 77km', which is about fifty miles, by which we calculated that we could reach the place, the oasis which was our final destination, in maybe two days, if we made good speed, and if the going was on packed dirt roads all the way.

In the evening we took down from the tree the bag in which we had hung our remaining fish. Part of the reason we had hung it there was to keep the insects off, but we had reckoned without the ingenuity of ants: a colony of them had found it out somehow, and a big army of them had spent the best part of the day making their way up the trunk, along the branch and down into the bag. By the time we discovered this, the fish was swarming with them. More than this, it had been affected by the heat, and had swollen up to the extent that its eyes had popped out.

We were, however, hungry.

I was still losing weight, and my ribs were beginning to stick out.

So what we did was to boil it for a bit longer than the previous day's fish.

It tasted vile, I remember, like eating a bar of soap.

We ate it anyway.

Andy had seconds.

The Still Point of the Turning World

There is, in this life, only one destination. We all get there, sooner or later.

I am stepping out of time here, for a moment, and jumping ahead of myself; but there came a time, some days later, when we were in a car, with Kibiriti driving, and Thesiger in the passenger seat, and we were going fast, far too fast, and Thesiger said, 'Kibiriti, what are you going to do with the time you've saved, when you get there?'

And when you get there, in the end, then there is nothing more to be done, and you either don't have what you want, or else, if you have, then it goes away again.

It is not, I think, in the destination where life is, but rather it is in the journey itself.

To step back, once more, into the flow of the narrative, and into fate of the small party of men and beasts making their way along the course of the Awash, all that time ago, then to this journey there was a destination, to be sure, and as they made camp at a place known as Gerumudli, on the edge of the forest that lay by a bend in the river in the shadow of the Magenta Mountains, they knew that their destination lay somewhere beyond, somewhere in the untracked deserts on the other side, past the furthest borders of the land of Aussa. But that night all of life, and all of time, were soon to become manifest then and there in the hush of a forest clearing lit by the moon's pale shine.

A messenger came first into the camp late in the afternoon, alone and on foot, saying that the Sultan himself was on his way, and that they should prepare themselves to greet him. This they did, and the camp was laid out as they would wish it to be seen, and boots and buckles polished, and the ground swept, and the soldiers lined up to greet their honoured guest.

Just before sunset the messenger came again.

Unfortunately, he said, there had been a change of plan.

The Sultan, regrettably, had with him far too many men to fit comfortably into the travellers' camp, and instead he had asked that they should come out to meet him where he was, which was in the forest close by.

So it was that they set off, dressed in their best clothes and carrying their rifles, and with the soldiers leading the way, into the dense forest, along narrow paths overgrown with creepers and through clearings covered ankle-deep with a bean-like clover that gave off a strange heavy smell when they walked upon it, while on all sides, through the foliage, they could see the watching eyes of warriors beyond number and the glint of spears and rifle-barrels, and they could hear the constant footsteps of runners arriving and departing.

Deeper and deeper they went, and still the woods around them were alive with watchers, until they came at last to a wide open clearing, encircled on all sides by tall trees. Before them, at the far side, stood some 400 warriors arranged into two great lines, all dressed in white and with filed teeth, and all carrying rifles and full belts of cartridges, and with long curved knives strapped across their stomachs.

And in the centre of these two lines, in a heavy carved wooden throne, sat the Sultan, surprisingly small in physical stature but grave and bearded in countenance, fine-boned and oval-faced, and dressed in finely woven robes of pure white, and wearing an ancient silver-hilted dagger. His hand rested on the handle of a silver-topped black stick, and behind his throne stood a band of slaves, all carrying rifles in red silk covers.

The Sultan rose, and with a wave of his hand he dismissed all his men except for an interpreter. Thesiger did the same, stepping forward across the clearing towards the throne and taking only Omar with him.

The moon had risen in the sky by this time, climbing high above the treetops and illuminating the scene below with the cold light reflected through space from its empty mountains and valleys.

This was it, and all in all.

'As I looked around the clearing,' wrote Thesiger,

'At the ranks of squatting warriors and the small isolated group of my own men, I knew that this moonlight meeting in unknown Africa with a savage potentate who hated Europeans was the realisation of my boyhood dreams. I had come here in search of adventure: the mapping, the collecting of animals and birds were all incidental. The knowledge that somewhere in this neighbourhood three previous expeditions had been exterminated, that we were far beyond any hope of assistance, that even our whereabouts were unknown, I found wholly satisfying.'

'You may begin,' said the Sultan, 'by telling me of your travels so far.'

A Surfeit of Shoes

It was a good day for walking, and a long day, consequently: the weather slightly overcast, though the hot wind still blew across the land.

We followed the road at first along the shores of Lake Turkana, and at one point we stopped and all went into the lake.

Our two Rendille, who could not swim, splashed and played at the edge, washing themselves and laughing, and the elder of them lay down and pushed himself along with his hands, pretending to swim.

The lake was the most beautiful green in colour, dark, deep green, and somewhat choppy with the wind.

As we swam, three Turkana women passing by stopped to watch us for a while. They were dressed in beaded loincloths, with long skin cloaks over their shoulders and backs, fastened around their necks with beaded straps, and their lower lips were pierced through with brass strips.

Thesiger had come this way, once, some thirty years before, when the area was known as the Northern Frontier District, and when it was still largely closed to outsiders, and he had worn a pair of fine, stout, handmade shoes. I do not remember which make they were now: Lobb, say, or from some such bespoke

London shoemaker: the sort of place where they carve a wooden last of your foot and keep it in store for when you come back for your next pair. His companion at the time had urged him to take a spare pair of shoes, in case those wore out. 'Nonsense,' he had said, 'absolute nonsense. I have had these shoes for thirty years' – or however long it was – 'and they haven't failed me yet! Look to your own shoes.' But fail him they did, and one of the soles came right away, and flapped constantly as he walked.

This, now, happened to me. Although my own shoes were considerably less fine and exclusive, and neither had any lasts, wooden or otherwise, been made for my feet, yet still they were, supposedly, tough. They were expensive American deck-shoes with thick leather uppers and the stitching they used to hold the uppers to the rubber soles was, they said, unbreakable. This stitching now broke and my right shoe came apart, right back to the middle of the foot. I do not know whether it was because of the heat or the rocky, volcanic soil or what the reason, but it flapped madly, and meant that I had to lift my foot conspicuously and place it down flat with every step, like a clown pretending to creep.

In the end Apa lent me a pair of sandals made of car-tyres until we stopped for lunch, and I got out a needle and a reel of thick button-thread and had a go at mending my shoe, while the Rendille looked on intently. It was not a good job that I made of it, but it was the only one I could, and it did me, for a while. The shoes had been made moccasin-style, with a single piece of leather beneath the foot and pulled up all around to make the sides. A leather midsole had been stitched on before the shoes had been closed up, and then a rubber outsole stuck on with glue afterwards. To restitch the thing properly I would have had to open the shoe up, prise off the outsole from the midsole, restitch the midsole, glue the outsole back on and then close the shoe back up.

I had a needle and a reel of button-thread.

And I had a stone – or any number of stones I fancied – to push the needle through.

What I did, in the circumstances, was to stitch a big loop through from the end of the rubber sole to the stitched welt at the top of the toe and pull it tight, and then repeat the process over and over again, so the sole was sort of tacked on at the toe. It gaped, but it didn't exactly flap.

Bloody hell.

The construction and repair of shoes. Sometimes you get very involved in these things, I think, when you've had to do them; and you don't necessarily realise quite how much time you've spent thinking or talking about them, or in quite how much detail. It's like those people who sometimes come up to you at parties, and go on at enormous length about the bus-route they had taken to get to there, and the stop they got on at and the stop they got off at, and the alternative route they might have taken if they'd caught a different bus to start with, and then changed, and the relationship of the time taken for the journey they actually took to the details published in the timetable. They always take buses, I find, these people. And they live at home with their mums.

Although, saying that, my first book – all a hundred and however many pages it was – was devoted entirely to the subject of weights and measures. And there was a big section in it on the relative merits of different ways of measuring out shoe-sizes, and a discussion of barleycorns versus Paris points as the base units of foot-measurement. So make of that what you will.

But anyway, I fixed my shoe.

It's not a big deal.

After this, the road left the lake shore and headed off across a barren, shadowless black volcanic plain. There were motor-vehicles on the road: five passed us that day; and, most times, their occupants stopped to talk to us. A diesel-powered Mercedes lorry came by, full of Germans. They'd had the thing flown in by transporter plane for their holiday. A Suzuki jeep brought two Italians; a bush-taxi, a *Matatu*, had a group of Turkana *moran* in the back. A British Army Land Rover came packed with Scottish soldiers in the tarpaulin-covered flatbed at the back. On exercises, they told us how, a few days before, on their way up the country they had come across an overturned lorry with the driver, thrown from his cab, laying dying in the road; and how, as he lay there, people were rifling through his pockets for anything that might be of value. They also told us how, on their unit's previous spell in Kenya, the men had been told on no account and under no circumstances to go with any of the prostitutes in Nairobi, because most of them had AIDS; but as soon as they were let out of their quarters men had gone with them, anyway, and, to nobody's great surprise, had caught it.

I don't know what you're meant to say to something like that.

Who knows what they had been thinking of, or whether, indeed, thinking had had much to do with anything at all.

We camped the night in a dry river-bed, and the camels, when we unloaded them, rolled and played in the gravel like puppies – or whatever the camel equivalent of a puppy is.

A *calf*, apparently.

The Giving and Receiving of Gifts

Having heard all that he wished to hear, the Sultan sat back in his throne.

'Return to this place tomorrow morning,' he said, 'and we shall discuss this matter further.'

They were escorted back through the moonlit forest by the vizier, together with a large party of warriors.

At a certain point in a smaller clearing on the way back to camp, the vizier stopped and clapped his hands, at which fourteen men emerged from the bushes, each carrying a heavy burden upon his shoulder.

'This,' said the vizier, 'is my master's gift to you.'

Twelve full skins of milk, there were, and two of ghee.

'He is very kind,' said Thesiger, 'and in return I have gifts for your master in my camp. They are poor in relation to these, but we are travellers and cannot bring with us all that we would wish.'

'My master will be most grateful to receive your gifts.'

They walked on, and as they went, the vizier told him a story.

Three Asaimara had come up from Bahdu, not one week before.

In the lands around the borders of Aussa they had met an old Adoimara and had made friends with him. He, in return, had invited them to his hut and introduced them to his wife and baby daughter, and although he was not a rich man he had feasted them with meat from his small flock of goats, and with milk, and with what little flour and other provisions he had. They had accepted his hospitality gratefully, and had stayed in his house for three days. Then, on the third day, they had said that he had been exceedingly kind but they must now, regretfully, go back to their homes. He had taken them as far as the path to Bahdu and had waved them off and wished them good speed.

Late that night, when the old man and his family were asleep, the three Asaimara had returned and, knowing where he slept, they had murdered him and all his family.

They were captured the next day, and were now in the Sultan's prison awaiting punishment.

'And by the way,' the vizier added, 'your companion Ahmado. He is from Bahdu, is he not?'

'He is . . .'

'His people are known to our people.'

He paused a moment, as if deep in thought.

'But he is, of course, our honoured guest. And now, I see, we are at your camp.'

The gift for the Sultan that Thesiger and his men brought to the clearing in the forest the next day was a sack of coffee too heavy for one man to carry, and four pots of sweet jelly – or rather, it would have been four but the Englishman had insisted on tasting them himself in front of the Sultan to make sure none was off, and in doing this he had dropped one of the pots and emptied its contents all over the ground.

'It is no matter,' said the Sultan. 'It is a sign of good luck.'

They sat, this time, in a tent erected in the clearing, and there they drank tea and coffee from white china cups and ate biscuits from dainty side-plates, served to them by white-clad battle-scarred men wearing long, curved daggers, with their teeth filed into fangs.

The Sultan, for such a small man, had an extraordinarily large appetite.

'I hear,' he said, taking another biscuit from his plate, 'that you have knowledge of medicine.'

'I have some little knowledge, sir.'

At a signal a slave was brought before them with a hand swollen like a balloon and seeping with white pus.

'He was bitten by a snake,' said the Sultan, 'some weeks ago.'

'I shall try my best to help him, sir.'

A man was sent to fetch the expedition medical kit and the Sultan sat back in his chair and watched, sipping at his coffee and eating yet more biscuits, as the Englishman lanced the swelling and squeezed out the thick pus, and then dusted the surface of the skin with a white patent powder from a packet, before wrapping the whole thing in a white crepe bandage and tying it off in a knot.

'Now,' said the Sultan, the entertainment over, 'to business.'

He was satisfied, he said, with the explanations he had received. As a consequence the party was to be allowed to pass through Aussa and into the lands beyond. For this space of time they would be accompanied by the royal vizier, who would bear with him the silver baton of command, to ensure that no one further up the river got the wrong idea about the Englishman. Or, indeed, about any of his companions. Accidents did happen, he said; and it would be most regrettable if anyone should take it into their head to do any harm to any particular member of the party. Whichever clan or family he might happen to come from.

As for the ultimate goal of the expedition, the Sultan did not, himself, know of the place where the river ended. It was not within his borders. He would make enquiries, but about their outcome he could not make any promises.

On returning to their camp, Thesiger and his companions found four white bulls tethered there. These, they were told, were a further gift from the Sultan. They also found a large party of heavily armed warriors camped little more than a hundred yards away.

No explanation was offered.

Ahmado took particular pains not to stray from the camp alone.

The Anticipation of Fruit

The desert became greener as we walked.

We had set off on a plain of black rocks, but little by little this gave way to sand, and then sand dotted with bushes, thorn bushes with leaves upon them, and then, at last, we left the black rocks behind. We saw gazelles and also many tracks of animals both large and small.

We stopped early for lunch because the land we had crossed had been hard on the camels. There had been no grazing for them all the previous day, and they were not happy about it, and not strong because of it. But today there was grazing.

Ahead on the horizon we could see the faint shape of two mountains, and it was there we were headed, to the place called South Horr, an oasis-settlement fed by a river, the end of our journey and somewhere where fruit of every kind imaginable was to be had.

Oranges, there were, and lemons. Bananas and papayas also.

We talked about these fruits while we ate our goat and *ugali*.

I had not eaten a papaya before, but Osman had, and he told us about the sweetness of the flesh and the juiciness: juiciness such that it runs down your face when you eat. Papaya, he said, was good to eat. He could eat many papayas.

Frazer, Andy and I were of the unanimous opinion that we could, too. Papayas sounded just the thing.

We would be at South Horr by lunchtime the following day, all being well.

Seven or eight hours of hard walking in the afternoon and evening took us to a dry river-bed with more bushes for the camels and there we made our camp for the night, and the Rendille cut thorn branches with their pangas and built a kraal for the camels, while I got out my needle and thread and had a second go at repairing my shoes, which were beginning to come apart again.

A short way from us a group of *moran* also had a camp with their cattle, and we could see the light of their fire long into the night and hear the sing-song note of their voices.

I fell asleep and dreamt of fruit.

Through the Land of Aussa

So it was that Thesiger and his party set off through Aussa itself, accompanied by the Sultan's vizier, Yaio, who carried the silver baton, and who was escorted by a group of warriors who were his guards and attendants.

Aussa was, for the most part, swamp and forest; thirty square miles of it surrounded by a ring of high mountains, inhabited by Danakil of both Asaimara and Adoimara bands, and teeming with warthog, and with leopard and hyena. When the rains came, each year, the waters of the swamp rose up and engulfed the forest, and the people and their herds moved up to the mountainsides until the waters subsided. It is not known where the warthog, leopard and hyena went at these times: perhaps they swam, or perhaps they climbed trees, or perhaps they found for themselves patches of high ground or places on the mountainsides where there were no people.

There were many villages in Aussa, and in them all feasting and dancing when the expedition passed through; and even where there were no villages there were constant gifts of animals and milk and ghee brought from the Sultan, carried to them by a constant stream of runners.

They ate well, and were well provided for.

In the villages there was, however, doctoring to be done, since the word had got about; and oftentimes the ailments were such that there was nothing to be done, and the cases hopeless and the suffering pitiful, and yet still there was the appearance of doctoring to be kept up, since it was expected.

'I had a man brought to me in the last stages of consumption,' wrote Thesiger, 'a living skeleton with his large burning eyes. There is little enough one can do for most of these people. Usually I give them something useless but harmless. I hate doing this, however, since they have such faith in you.'

At the far side of this swamp and forest the river flowed out into open land, where herds of black, hump-backed cattle with swept-back half-moon horns grazed at the water's edge. The river flowed onward to the far mountain wall and descended, through a series of terrifying gullies and precipices, into flat land beyond. In this further land past the mountain wall, the river spread out through beds of high, tufted reeds, and then flowed on into a chain of wide shallow lakes, alive with hordes of crocodiles and hippos, and surrounded all about by soft mud, over which the going was slow and difficult.

There were also, during this time, various difficulties with insects. There was a plague of bluebottles in the camp one day, covering the men and animals and also their food when they tried to eat. There were tarantulas found in tents, some as big as your hand. There were scorpions discovered – too late – in clothing, and there was stinging and swelling in consequence.

Also a pair of good, handmade English shoes came apart with the constant wet, and had to be stitched back together again.

Eventually, though, they reached a lake that was bigger than all of the others and no outlet to the waters could be seen at the far side.

'This,' said Yaio, 'is where the river ends.'

But the water was fresh, not salt.

If the river had ended there, and simply evaporated, year after year, then it would have been salt.

'There must be an exit,' said Thesiger

'There is not,' said the vizier.

But upon climbing a small escarpment to overlook the scene, it was discovered that there was, indeed, an exit, a concealed mouth on the southern shore, from which the Awash led away through two more lakes and then passed into a great swamp beyond.

Omar, meanwhile, had been making a number of enquiries, and had discovered from members of the escort that they knew of this exit and these lakes and this swamp, and of a further lake beyond, foul and evil-smelling, in the burning desert down by the border of Issa country. This was a place where, one told Omar in confidence, the Sultan was not to keen for them to go, on account of the situation with that tribe, and on account of the sensitive matter of the precise delineation of borders.

Thesiger, however, was adamant.

Eventually, it was agreed that runners should be sent back to the Sultan to ask his permission. Two days later they came back saying that they could proceed, if they so wished, but that it might be better if they were to choose a different route.

Thesiger's decision, however, was to press on, and he would not be swayed.

Yaio's warriors then went into a huddle and announced that if the Englishman insisted on going that way, then they would escort him.

Yaio rode back to inform the Sultan in person of this fact, telling the others to set off on their way, and promising to meet them again at a further point.

This he did, returning some days later bringing with him from the Sultan a gift of five oxen and a dozen skins of milk.

Thesiger was overwhelmed at the generosity of the man and his people, even though, with his insistence on pursuing the river to its end, he had been pushing hard against the limits of their tolerance.

'They may be a murderously inclined race,' he wrote, 'but no one would call them inhospitable.'

Shortly afterwards, on the edge of the wide and barren desert across which they must go to reach the further lake, Yaio announced that he needed, at last, to return to his home, and he handed the silver baton over to the senior of his headmen, and wished them all well.

Thesiger presented him with a rifle and assured him once again that he would never do anything to harm the Sultan or his people.

To which Yaio replied that he had realised this, as had the Sultan.

That was why they had agreed to help, and it was why the expedition was where it was, and why Thesiger and his men were still alive, rather than laying hacked to pieces somewhere as might so easily have been the case under other circumstances.

It was why, conversely, the previous expeditions had ended up as they had, having been acting as agents, largely, of outside powers, and having been concerned with military objectives, or with the mapping of borders not necessarily to Aussa's advantage.

With this he took his leave, and turned about and set off back to the land of forest and swamp beyond the mountains that was Aussa.

For those who stayed, all that remained now was to reach the final lake.

Or rather, all that remained now was to reach the final lake, and then to push on for however long it took and to make their way across however many miles of desert lay between them and the coast at Djibouti; and to trust that their water and their supplies held out for the duration – or else that they should be able to obtain more along the way. This was by no means certain.

The Oasis

The land became steadily greener as we walked.

We came to a shallow river, trees on either bank, which we crossed at a ford. A small monkey, basking lazily by the water's edge, scampered up into the branches of a tree at our approach.

On the other side of the river the path led towards a stand of wide-spaced trees, and from these a huge herd of camels emerged, being driven by a group of Rendille.

Big eyes, the young camels had, and a skittish manner about them as they came on their way. We stopped, our party and the Rendille party, and our own Rendille exchanged news with them. Relatives of Apa, no doubt: all the other Rendille we had met seemed to be, so I do not see why these should have been any exception. And we bought from them milk, camel's milk, and drank it from the big gourd they held out to us for that purpose. It tasted very rich and full – though how much of that was due to the poverty of our diet in the days before I do not know – and also it had a taste of smoke to it, wood-smoke. This, I think, may have been from the gourd from which we drank it.

When we had finished we bade the camel-herders goodbye and walked the short distance to the oasis-settlement of South Horr.

Though all the land around is desert, South Horr is almost alpine – a green place, surrounded by green mountains, and the sound of cow-bells in the air all about.

We went to the garden of an eating-house, which was also a slaughterhouse and a butcher's shop, and there we ate a lunch of meat with boiled potatoes and flour chapattis at a table by the edge of a stream that flowed down from one of the mountains, from which we filled and refilled our cups with water, which tasted very good and very sweet.

There were trees overhanging, and big yellow flowers upon them, and birds with plumed heads and long tails that sat and ate the flowers.

The village in the oasis sat on the border between the lands of the Rendille and those of the Samburu and the people there, consequently, were of both tribes, with a few Somalis thrown in for good measure.

Osman, who was Samburu, pointed to one of the mountains above the village, the one from which the clear stream flowed, and said that high on its slopes there lay a cave, called KosiKosi, which was home to a great spirit and which was sacred to his people. They believe, he said, that wherever in the country they may happen to be, KosiKosi sits always at the centre of their world.

And, he said, beyond the mountain of the sacred cave there lay a desert valley where the Turkana believe that many devils live.

We found a place on the edge of the village and made our camp, where we would wait for Kibiriti to arrive, and to take us then to the home of Wilfred Thesiger.

Fulfilment's Desolate Attic

They came upon the lake much sooner than they expected.

It was an evil-smelling place.

A vast sheet of thick, soapy green water, the lake was; many miles wide, dotted with sheets of red algae, and surrounded all about by flats of unstable black mud, through which jutted white salt reefs and the salt-encrusted remains of dead trees. Great clouds of small, hard-bodied midges swarmed all around.

It took several days for the party to circumnavigate the lake, such was its size, and such the difficulty of the ground all around; but circumnavigate it they did, though they were plagued constantly by the midges. On one day they were assaulted by a violent sandstorm. On another they passed the spot where, the Danakil guides said, the Swiss mercenary Munzinger and his party had been massacred nearly sixty years before.

There was no outlet to the waters of the lake.

There was, instead, only a constant pouring-in of river-water and a constant evaporation into the hot air; a gradual accretion, year by year, of the salts and sediments borne down by the Awash on its journey from the highlands of Abyssinia.

This place, and no other, was the river's final destination.

And that was it.

'I had come far,' wrote Thesiger, 'and risked much to see this desolate scene.'

There was nothing more to be done in that place.

The next day they set off for the French post at Aseila on the Gobald plain, where they could expect to find food and drink and grazing for the camels, which, after four days by that lifeless lake and the journey across the hot desert to reach it, had now become worryingly weak.

But it was not far, the guides said, no more than three hours away, at the most.

Consequently they travelled light, carrying little water with them to make the going easier and faster for the animals.

But they were wrong about the distance and wrong about the time it would take them to cover it.

It took not three hours but three days, and before long the camels were in a very bad way indeed. To make it easier on them they took to resting up by day and travelling in the cool of the night, but by the second day things had reached the point where two of the animals had collapsed and lay slowly dying in the sand. In the end they had to be shot.

This was painful for all of the party, and not least because all of their lives depended upon the creatures. For the handlers, meanwhile, who knew each of their animals individually by name and character and lineage, it was little short of a tragedy.

On the third day they reached the French post, which was strongly fortified to fight off attacks from Adoimara, Asaimara and Issa, all of whom claimed the territory. There they were welcomed by a Corsican called Antoniali and his garrison of sixty Somalis. At this place, after eating, drinking and resting the night, Ali, Ahmado and the Sultan's men all said their goodbyes, and, suitably rewarded, they set off back to Aussa.

The remainder of the expedition stayed at the post for three days and three nights before setting off into the desert again, heading for the next French fort, at Dikil, which was even more strongly fortified, with glass-topped walls twenty feet high and two machine-gun towers, and which was commanded by the Commandant de Cercle, Captain Bernard, who lived there with his wife and child. Here the Abyssinian soldiers were paid off with a large gift of money and it was arranged for them to be sent by lorry to Alisabiet, from whence they would return by train to Abyssinia.

Captain Bernard fed and housed the remaining members of the expedition for three days, and than arranged for his adjutant, Dongradi, and an escort of twelve soldiers, together with their own camels and a machine gun, to escort them over the desert on the last leg of their journey.

He was a kind man, Captain Bernard, though in the end he suffered for his kindness. Some eight months later he heard that a party of Issa were being threatened by a far larger band of Asaimara, 1,200 strong. He went out to help, but the Asaimara, having killed the Issa, then turned on him. He and his entire garrison – including his wife and child – were killed and their bodies horribly mutilated.

The expedition and its escort of French Somali troops set off across the desert, aiming to make regular stops for water and grazing along the way. The weather, however, had been cruel there and in all of the places they expected to find water there was none; neither was there grazing of any kind. For five days and nights this continued, and again, and one by one, more camels began to falter and die.

On the fifth day they came to a great salt-pan many miles across in a depression 500 feet below sea-level; and there, in the middle of it all, and in the midst of the fiercest heat any of them had known, was a wide blue lake. But when they approached the lake something about it did not seem quite right, for around it there were no signs of life of any kind: not a bird, not a lizard, not even a fly or any insect.

The water was all salt and wholly undrinkable.

At this point they began to unpack the camels, and to discard anything and everything in their equipment that they could do without.

They walked on again, and as they walked, and as their situation worsened, they stopped and discarded more.

Yet more camels died.

Eventually they reached a water-hole; but by this time only four of the original nineteen camels with which they had left Awash Station were left

'It was heartbreaking,' wrote Thesiger, 'for I knew them all so well; among others little Farur, Elmi, Hansiya and great-hearted Nagadras, who always led the caravan.'

On the next day they saw, in the distance, the desert's edge; and beyond it, far off, the blue of the sea.

A day later they reached the coast, at Tajura.

It was now six full months since the expedition began.

Then things happened quickly. There was a meeting with the Sultan of Tajura, and feasting and dancing, and a tour of the Sultan's palace with a viewing of the modern refrigerator newly installed in its kitchens.

There was a crossing by dhow to Djibouti, and a rather less enthusiastic welcome from the French Commandant, Chapon Baisac, a 'corpulent, pompous and short-tempered little man' who demanded to know on whose authority, precisely, the Englishman had had the effrontery to bring armed Abyssinian soldiers into French territory.

And then there was the purchase a single one-way ticket for a third-class cabin on a Messageries Maritimes boat bound for Marseilles.

Omar walked with Thesiger to the docks and accompanied him on board, where they shook hands and said goodbye; and the headman then made his way back down the gangplank, past the passengers still embarking with their suitcases and their sunhats, and disappeared into the crowds milling on the quay. They never saw each other again.

From Marseilles Thesiger took the sleeper-train to Paris, and from there a further train to Calais, and then a ferry to Dover.

And a chapter of his life closed behind him, never to open again.

Back to Maralal

What else do I remember of the oasis-settlement of South Horr?

A boy with fever brought before us, and him shivering so much that we could hear the chattering of his teeth, and us giving the man who brought him to us our remaining packets of malaria tablets.

And the food, again, and being overcharged horribly for it.

And saying goodbye to our Rendille camel-men, who left to return to their homes and their people.

And Kibiriti coming late in the morning, having spent the night before in Baragoi, and driving us back to Maralal.

'Tomorrow,' he said, 'Wilfred will be here. But before that, we will have much goat!'

'Actually,' said Andy, 'if it's all the same with you, we'll give the goat a miss. Just for today.'

Civilisation

The seed of a mesquite tree took root, once, in the desert by the shores of Lake Turkana. Sensing water deep beneath the sand and rocks, it sent down its long tap-root low into the ground to where, a hundred feet or more below, this water was to be found. Slowly, slowly, over the years, the tree began to grow; not tall, for this was not a place for tall trees, but it sent up its branches towards the sky and it spread down its roots all around. And as it grew, and as its roots forced their way further into the earth, so they turned over and turned up some of the things that lay beneath. And presently there appeared, at the base of the tree's trunk, some small splinters of bone, too old and too dry for the scavengers to pay any attention to; and so they lay there, for day after day, for month after month and for year after year, until, one day, a man found them and picked them up. They were odd, these bones, and hard and stone-like, and not at all like the bones of any animal that he had seen.

And it happened that these bones, eventually, found their way into the hands of an anthropologist.

Four years later, after an extraordinarily protracted and pain-staking excavation, this anthroplogist and his companions managed to recover and to reconstruct, from the ground beneath

213

the mesquite tree, the skeleton of an 11- or 12-year-old boy, almost entire. He was five foot three, this boy, when he died, and was likely to have reached six feet or thereabouts had he lived, or so they calculated. And he had died one and a half million years before.

A decade later, in the Samburu Hills just outside Maralal, twenty fossil fragments were discovered – mainly scraps and shards of teeth and jawbones, they were, but they were older by far than the Lake Turkana boy, and were the remains, perhaps, of mankind's oldest and most distant ancestors.

And over the years we scattered and spread far and wide over the face of the earth.

Ten thousand years ago, when the ice-sheets retreated, we left our caves made a life for ourselves as hunters and foragers in the plains and the forests. And that suited us just fine: it suited us fine for a long while. But little by little, over time, things began to change.

In the open lands, in Africa, the hunters of wild sheep and goats gradually became herders and pastoralists, as the Samburu and Rendille are today, and went from following their quarry's migrations between their seasonal pastures to leading them there and protecting them from other predators with their spears and bows, and increasing the size of their flocks.

Further north, a wave of settlers from the Near East crossed the sea and landed on the Greek coast. These people were not hunters and gatherers; nor were they pastoralists and herders. They were the first farmers, and they brought with them tools and techniques for clearing and transforming the land, and for the sowing and reaping of crops.

They lived a hard life, these farmers, and one of constant, grinding labour, in which they would work for months on end with little immediate reward; and their manner of living was unenvied by the indigenous hunters, and mostly ignored, for nigh on a thousand years.

Little by little, however, the farmers' settlements began to spread northwards and westwards across Europe's plains and the river-valleys, and so successful were they that their methods, in time, came to be imitated by my ancestors and by Wilfred Thesiger's, and perhaps by yours; and they all, in time, came to spend their days tilling the land with stone hoes.

In return for giving up a life of comparative leisure for one of hard manual work, the settled farmers were both rewarded and penalised.

They were rewarded, on the one hand, by conditions that led, in time, to civilisation, to the world's great empires, and, ultimately, to the Industrial Revolution and to the world we live in today.

And on the other hand, and more immediately and tangibly, they were penalised with a decline in both the quality and quantity of their lives over those of their hunting ancestors by every observable measure.

For the average person, the shift to settled farming brought with it a lower material income, a dramatic loss of leisure-time and a marked reduction in physical health, compared with their hunter-gatherer and pastoralist cousins, as measured both through stature and through life-expectancy. And this was not just for a transitional period of a few years or a few hundred or even a few thousand, but for more or less the whole of recorded history, right up until the dawn of the nineteenth century.

In 1800, the daily wage of an English farm-labourer would buy eleven pounds of wheat. He probably would have had other things to spend it on, mind; but if it was wheat that he wanted, then that was how much of it he would have got. But in ancient Babylon, in 1800 BC, the daily wage of a farm-labourer would have bought fifteen pounds of wheat. And in classical Athens it would have

215

bought twice as much. The English farm-labourer would have eaten other things besides wheat, though. With the wages from his ten-hours-a-day, 300-days-a-year job, he would have been able to afford, in a typical day, some hunks of bread and a little cheese to go with it, with perhaps some bacon-fat as well, and he would have washed it all down with some cups of weak tea, and also some beer. All of this, put together, would have given him about 1,500 calories-worth of nourishment. Whereas the daily food intake of the average hunter-gatherer, working just three hours a day, both then and now, and in all the tens of thousands of years before the first farmers arrived in Europe, was and is around 2,300 calories, and it is far more varied and far richer in protein besides.

So by farming the land instead of foraging and hunting in it or leading their herds across it to their seasonal pastures, people became poorer in terms of what they could afford to feed themselves, and this despite them working so much harder and so much longer.

And besides this, the new manner of living changed both the culture and the composition of the people. Because the qualities and attitudes that make you good and successful at lounging about for days painting yourself with war-paint, and then seeing off a leopard that's prowling around your camp or grabbing your spear and launching yourself off after a wild pig at half a second's notice, and then feasting until you're too fat to move, are not at all the same as the qualities and attitudes that make you good and successful at ploughing a field with a stick and scattering the good seed on the land, and then feeding and watering and weeding it day after day, and keeping the birds off, and weeding some more, all in anticipation of a harvest that could be half a year away or more – if the weather holds and if the rains don't fail. In that sort of life, the farming life, you tend to get a higher proportion of serious, duty-driven individuals with a strong work-ethic, who go in for deferred gratification and who are well suited to performing simple, repetitive tasks for hours, days, weeks and months on end.

Or, to be technical about this for a moment, you get a lot of the sort of people who inherit genes for what neuroscientists call a 'strong response inhibition mechanism in the dorsolateral prefrontal cortex', which is something that makes them better at being conscientious, organised, disciplined and self-controlled, and not so good at being spontaneous or acting on impulse. The sort of people, in fact, who at another time might be content to spend their whole lives sorting cheques into account-number order, or else training all hours to be good at a sport that they don't actually enjoy, because it's wrong to quit things.

But apart from turning out the puritans and pedants of the future, one thing that settled farming did do very well indeed was to vastly increase the number of people that the land could support, and wherever farming took hold the population exploded. This meant that eventually, by sheer weight of numbers, the new people swallowed up the old and the new way of living replaced the old way altogether.

And from there it was not such a big step to the cotton mills.

That's progress for you, though. And that's civilisation.

The Years In Between

'I had no desire to go back to civilisation,' he had said, 'and wished I was just starting out from the Awash Station with the whole Awash River still before me to explore.'

There are some that see life as a matter of departures – a process of moving on and leaving behind, of exploration and discovery.

And there are others that see it all as one long, circuitous return-trip, the aim of which, always, is to get back home; and in so doing to regain what was lost and what left behind, and so to arrive, once more, at the place where you know that you belong, among the people whom you recognise, at last, as your own people, and there to become what you really are and always were.

And I cannot for the life of me say which of the two it was that had the upper hand in the life of the man.

There were departures, to be sure, and more departures than most.

He was not long back in England. A while in The Milebrook, his mother's home on the Welsh borders, and the village with its post office and its pub and its church and church hall, and the river that ran shallow on its stony bed through the green valley beside; and then it was down to London, by steam-train, and the lectures at the Royal Geographical Society, and the unfinished language-course at the School of Oriental and African Studies.

Then he went to the Sudan, first as a colonial administrator, an Assistant District Commissioner in Darfur, and then as a junior officer, or Bimbashi, in the Defence Force.

War followed and he left the Sudan to fight against the Italians in Abyssinia; then to Syria, to fight with the Druze Legion against the Vichy French; and from there to the Western Desert with the newly formed SAS, to fight the Germans, and rising there to the rank of major.

In the years that followed the war, others returned to their homes, picked up the pieces of interrupted careers and marriages, re-entered, as best they could, the half-gone childhoods of children who had more than half-forgotten what they had ever looked like.

But for him there were more departures still.

To Arabia, there to live and travel with the Bedouin.

To Iraq, there to spend some seven years, on and off, in the reed longhouses of the Marsh Arabs.

And the books he wrote about those years and the photographs he took, and the acclaim that followed.

And after, to Kurdistan, to Afghanistan, to the Hindu Kush and the Karakoram, to Morocco. To more fighting, still, on the side of the Royalists and against the communists in the Yemeni civil war.

Then four expeditions, through the borderlands of Uganda, the Sudan and Kenya. During which he made a crossing of the deserts of the Northern Frontier District, climbing Mount Kulal and exploring the shores of Lake Turkana.

In all these places he saw, and recorded in his writings, the last days of ancient worlds and ways of life that were themselves in the process of departing from the world; and which, today, are mostly all gone. Long gone.

These were, indeed, departures.

And yet, running through them all like the waters of a river moving ever onwards through the changing landscape of his life there was also a constant longing for what had once been; a yearning to return to the life of ancient and savage nobility that he had once seen, in earlier days, in the sun-scorched land of his birth, and also, at another time, in pale moonlight glinting on spear-points in a clearing in a wood on the borders of the forbidden kingdom of Aussa.

And now these times were all gone and he had washed up here, where I was, in the little town of Maralal, with his three adopted 'sons', and with their people; who, much of the time called him, simply, The Old Man, Up There.

The Old Man, Up There

We were sitting outside Mr Bhola's garage in Maralal watching the world go by and drawing figures in the dirt with our sticks when we heard the roar of the engine and the grating of the gears and saw the Land Cruiser coming towards us. It came at speed, jolting and bumping over the potholes of the town street, and it sent up a cloud of dust in its wake, and scattered the people in its path; and there was a figure in the passenger-seat, turning to gesticulate at the driver and then looking towards where we sat and pointing; and then the car screeched to a halt before us and Wilfred Thesiger stepped out. Or rather, he half-stepped out, but he hadn't yet done with what he was saying.

'How often do I have to tell you, Kibiriti?' he said, 'How often?'

Kibiriti grinned and shrugged and said nothing.

'You'll kill us all one day. You see if you don't.'

And then he turned towards where we stood, lined up like an honour-guard, having hastily jumped to our feet and wiped the dust from our hands on our shorts.

'So,' he said, 'you survived.'

He had on the same tweed suit that he had worn when I had met him in Tite Street, despite the heat, and a green canvas hat with a soft brim, of the kind worn by fishermen; and he carried a carved walking-stick of dark wood.

We rose to our feet and shook hands with him, awkwardly, formally.

Andy had a battered paperback copy of *Arabian Sands* in his left hand when he stepped forward, and Thesiger spotted it.

'Well, what do you think of it?' he said, nodding towards the book.

And Andy, overawed, stammered something about it having been excellent, although he hadn't quite finished it yet; at which Thesiger grunted with satisfaction.

'Good,' he said. 'Now, what about a drink?'

And without waiting for an answer he strode purposefully across the road towards a tin-roofed shack with a tin Coca-Cola sign outside, and we scuttled along after him.

The shop-owner spotted him just before he crossed the threshold, and hastily switched off the transistor radio, from which a Michael Jackson tune had been blaring.

'Here,' said Thesiger, putting both hands on the counter before him and springing up upon it so that he was sitting facing us, 'three bottles of Coca-Cola for my young guests.'

He looked down at us, kicking the heels of his stout brown shoes against the wood as he counted out the coins into the palm of his hand and placed them down on the counter by his side.

'They say that I shouldn't do this sort of thing at my age. But I tell them: I'm eighty years old and if I can't do it now, then when can I ever? You tell me that, I say, you just tell me.'

We drank our drinks then and there, in the shop; being forbidden by the shop-owner to take our drinks outside, on account of there being a refundable deposit with the wholesaler on the bottles.

He had us tell him about our journey, as we drank, and he laughed when we told him about our meal of swollen fish, and again at our confusion over sheep and goats. Although, he said, he did not generally do so, as he was well known to have no sense of humour.

'Twice in one day is more than enough. They'll think I'm ill or something. But do you know how you tell the difference, eh? Between a sheep and a goat? Shall I tell you? Well, if the tail goes up, then it's a goat. And if it goes down, it's a sheep. That's how you tell. That's how I've always done it, and it works every time.'

We told him also about our constant thirst, and our endless discussions, while we walked, about lemonade, and what else we would drink, one day.

'Here's a trick for you,' he said. 'It's something the Bedu taught me. If you have no water, and no prospect of getting any, then you should put a little salt in the palm of your hand, like so, and then you lick it. That will help keep the thirst away.'

He caught sight of the camera slung around my neck.

'That's not one of those automatic things, is it?'

It was a rather large and clunky East German device, with a shutter that had a recoil to it which, I swear, was almost like a rifle.

'No,' I said, 'it's manual. Or else if you want you can have it half-automatic – see this dial here: you can set the aperture and it will do the shutter-speed for you.'

'Hmm . . . well, it's good you can use your own settings. I can't bear those fully automatic ones, the ones that do everything for you. You may as well not be there if you're going to do that. Put the thing on a rock and come back later when it's taken the pictures for you, you may as well. What film are you using, by the way?'

'A mixture. But I've got black and white in it now. Ilford 100ASA.'

'That's good,' he said, 'I've always preferred black and white to colour. It gives room to the imagination. It's the same with painting – I'd have a sketch over an oil-painting any day.'

He quizzed Andy on *Arabian Sands* again, and then asked Frazer and myself about our own reading. Frazer had been reading *A Short Walk in the Hindu Kush* by Eric Newby – who, as it happened, had come across Thesiger on his travels in the 1950s, and who, with his companion, had been castigated by him for sleeping on an air-bed instead of on the rocky ground. 'God,' he'd said, 'you must be a couple of pansies.'

I said that I'd been reading *The Adventures of Huckleberry Finn*.

'Who?' he said.

'*Huckleberry Finn*,' I said. 'You know. By Mark Twain.'

'Never heard of him,' he said.

Nor was he particularly interested in hearing about him.

He was not a great admirer of the Americans, he said.

He never had been, not even at the best of times. But it was Suez, I think, that put the tin lid on it.

It was in the Fifties. He was in Arabia at the time, just across the way, as it were, when the Egyptians decided to flex their muscles by taking control of the Suez Canal.

This caused havoc with the cargo ships passing between the Mediterranean and the Indian Ocean, and so the old colonial powers, Britain and France, joined together with Israel to invade and set the waterway free, and they looked to America to back them up.

America had its own fish to fry, though, and was busy with the Cold War, and consequently was having none of it. More than this, the Americans pressured the European allies into a humiliating climbdown.

This loss of territory and loss of face to a former colony marked the beginning of the final winding-down of the British Empire, and kicked off four decades of flag-lowering to the sounds of bugles playing the 'Last Post', which culminated in the return of Hong Kong to the Chinese.

It marked the end of Thesiger's time in Arabia, too: in the shifting political climate he was forced to leave; and he wasn't overly happy about that.

It marked something of a crisis in my own family, besides, though I had not yet been born. My father had not long left the army. He and my mother were living in my grandmother's rented two-bedroom bungalow, along with his uncle, and he was called up again and shipped out; and then, when it all went wrong, he was sent back home again. One of the first things he did when he got back was to go to the council offices to see how his long-standing application for a home of his own was doing.

'Now,' said the clerk, consulting his ledger, 'you were nearly at the top of the list, weren't you? Last time you came in.'

'That's right.'

'But it says here that you left the borough.'

'I was called up. For Suez.'

'Which means, when you look at it, that you've been living elsewhere.'

'Well, yes . . .'

'And if you've been living elsewhere, then what that means is you've got to start at the bottom of the list again.'

'What?'

'Well, you can't just come back in now, can you? In front of all the people who've been waiting here all along.'

'I was called up to risk my *life* for people like you.'

'Well,' said the clerk, 'there it is.'

How much the novels of Mark Twain have to do with any of this I don't know. Not a lot, I should imagine.

We changed the subject.

We spent much of that day together, talking about travel – or rather listening to him telling us about his travels, or else we sat outside Mr Bhola's garage watching the people of Maralal.

I took a photograph of him sitting there, leaning on his stick, with Frazer and Andy sitting on either side of him.

A party of Samburu *moran* with spears and ochred hair stopped a little way from where we sat.

'These Samburu,' he said, pointing with his stick, 'and all the other tribes of their kind – the Turkana, the Rendille, the Masai – they're *Nilotic*, the word is.' He told us how, it is believed, these tribes all made their way down the Nile centuries ago – or maybe even millennia; and how the language they speak comes from a family you can still hear today in some parts of Egypt. Over to the west there were the Luo and the Dinka, and they were Nilotic, too. And incidentally, he said, the Turkana: those clay-covered caps they wear on the back of their heads contain not only their own hair drawn back into a bun, but also the hair of their fathers, grandfathers and ancestors as well.

And suchlike things.

He stayed with us for much of the day.

He was glad of our company, he said.

And besides, he said, there was no one at home.

There was, he said, no great pleasure to be had in sitting alone in an empty room at his age.

Life

Lawi Leboyare was the eldest of Thesiger's 'sons'.

He was a man of some importance in Maralal, and had a house which had electricity in it; and which, in addition to electricity, had both a television and a video-recorder. He also owned a smart motor-car, despite Kibirit's best efforts to wreck it; and he had a great many cattle, and people to look after them, as well as a number of wives from the more sought-after and fashionable parts of the region.

Behind them all, in no little part, was the same generosity that had once brought me my cheque for 300 pounds and my injunction not to tell others.

It was to his house that we were invited for dinner on the night before our departure. Kibiriti and Laputa, his 'brothers', were invited, too, and Thesiger was there both as guest of honour and, in a manner of speaking, as the evening's entertainment; for after a large and hearty meal of goat stew, served up with boiled vegetables and chapattis, the lights were turned off, the television tuned on and a video-cassette removed from its box and placed into the slot of the machine. Then, to the strains of Vivaldi's Flute Concerto and over a background of spear-carrying Samburu *moran* running in slow-motion, the opening titles rolled, and there began

The Last Explorer, a documentary, recorded from British television, about Thesiger's life and times.

I do not know who had recorded it or who brought it out to this place.

It was a strange experience, that evening.

Partly it was strange on account of having the real thing in the room with us, commenting loudly on the commentary while it was commenting on him ('Nonsense! I never said that. You'll vouch for me, won't you, Lawi?').

It was also strange on account of the television authorities in the UK having just decided to allow the advertising of sanitary towels and tampons, as a result of which the entire industry seemed to have collectively come to the decision that the best way to exercise their new freedom and show all their product-demonstration shots of blue liquid being poured from laboratory flasks and then absorbed and locked in with a special new double action, was to blow the whole year's budget in one go and show them all, repeatedly, in every single ad-break in the Wilfred Thesiger documentary.

Or so it seemed.

Later that night, when the evening was over and we were about to make our way back to our hut for the last time, we parted with handshakes and with many thanks for the great kindness that had been shown to us.

'You will come again?' he said. 'Next time you can take donkeys and go to the forest.'

We never did.

I don't know why.

I always intended to, and, looking back on it now, and given my time again, I would have.

But I did not.

Life, I think: life gets in the way, sometimes, and then before you know it, it's all gone.

The bus came before dawn, pulling up right outside the hut where we slept.

It had been rerouted, that day, especially for us.

Kibiriti helped us load our things on board, and waved goodbye.

And then we were off, back across the wide open land.

To the Modern World

To Nairobi. To a city of two and a half million people and growing, where the modern world has brought with it an airport, and cars and buses, and offices and shops, and electric lighting in the streets at night. And where it has also brought with it the opportunity for a population explosion of extraordinary proportions, in which unprecedented numbers of people are able to live out their lives at ever-greater densities while their income levels plummet, and while their living-conditions deteriorate to an extent which, before the advent of industrialisation and modern medicine, would have been unthinkable and unsustainable.

In the Nairobi shanty-town of Kibera, once a forest settlement in which plots were awarded to Nubian soldiers in reward for their service in the First World War, upwards of a million people now live in shacks made of mud, boxes, polythene sheets and corrugated iron. Many draw their water from the choleric Nairobi dam and dispose of their bodily waste by tying it up it in plastic bags which they fling from the windows of their shacks to land wherever they will. There is little work to go around there, and what little there is pays next to nothing. There are always plenty of others desperate to do the job for the money, however small, if you turn your nose up at it. There is little else to do, apart from passing the time getting drunk on *changaa*, a potent illicit brew of around 50 per cent pure alcohol, which, for more 'kick' and for a semblance of greater potency, is often spiked with methanol. Or jet-fuel. Or battery-acid. Besides the *changaa*, and to a large extent because of it, there is crime and there is disease in the shanty-town, and people die, and die young. But they are born in greater numbers still, and for every one who leaves the world before his time there are two who come into it. A full half of the population there now are children – and still the population grows, though the place is now already more crowded than almost anywhere else on earth.

And from Nairobi, to London. To a city where rivers that once flowed through tree-lined fields now lie buried in iron pipes beneath the streets of workday traffic and where railway stations are built over them. To a city where many live in houses where, instead of spending ten minutes washing the dishes after eating your meal, you can spend just five minutes scraping them off and loading them into a special machine, and then drop a tablet into a holder inside the door, and then close the door and switch the machine on, and wait a couple of hours while the machine washes the dishes, and then after that you just need to spend five more minutes unloading the machine and putting the dishes away. And while the machine's doing your washing-up for you, you can do other things, or you can do nothing, just as you wish.

In the country where I live there were once wolves in the mountains.

There are none there now.

What Is Your Tribe?

It was not long after the end of the film in Lawi's house that the conversation came around to the subject of death, for some reason. I don't recall quite why, now, or what had led to it: my memory slips a little, twenty years on.

'When I go,' Thesiger said, 'I don't want some clergyman muttering mumbo-jumbo over me.'

He looked around him.

'No,' he said, 'I'd rather be left out for the jackals. But *they* won't hear of it, though.'

He motioned to Lawi, Laputa and Kibiriti.

'So as a compromise they've agreed to bury me in the garden here.'

The three 'sons' looked at each other and grinned.

'He is a very big man, this Wilfred,' said Lawi. 'He will need much digging.'

But he always thought, back then, that this is what would happen, in the end: he would end his days there in Maralal, and his three boys would bury him.

It didn't work out quite that way.

It began with Laputa.

In September 1994, quite suddenly, the young man fell ill and then died, aged just thirty-two.

Lawi, meanwhile, had grown ever more insistent in his need for money. He needed it, he said, for various necessary things, but these things somehow never seemed to materialise, no matter how much money he was given to buy them with. And he began to drink heavily.

And Kibiriti, with his wives in other towns, now had children of his own to raise, and, though he spent as much time with Thesiger as he could, his life was such that he was frequently busy elsewhere.

Thesiger returned to London, to his empty flat in Tite Street, and stayed there, alone, considering what to do next.

In April 1995, seven months after Laputa's death, Mr Bhola telephoned from his garage in Maralal to say that Lawi had suffered a stroke, brought on by his drinking, and had died.

A short while later Mr Bhola himself died.

Thesiger did not return.

And, meanwhile, his eyesight had begun to deteriorate. He had always been a great reader and had collected many books over the years, but now he found it increasingly slow and frustrating to attempt to read.

In November that year, he was knighted at Buckingham Palace by His Royal Highness the Prince of Wales; but around that time his right hand began to shake so much that he found it hard to write. The doctors diagnosed him as suffering the first stages of Parkinson's disease.

His eyesight, now, had become so bad that his books were of no further use to him, and he gave them all away, so that his flat, once so full of them, now had, instead, row upon row of empty shelves.

A short while later he moved from this flat to an old people's home in Coulsdon in Surrey, run by the Friends of the Elderly, where he was given a room overlooking the lawn.

In 2001 he began to be treated for Alzheimer's as well as Parkinson's.

He began to lose his memory, and the shaking of his hands, which had been kept largely under control through drugs, began to return. He began, also, to dribble. This caused him great distress.

As the months went by, his eyesight began to deteriorate still further, so that he found it difficult even to tell the time. He also began, at this time, to experience hallucinations. The building across the lawn from his window would appear to expand and contract, while men in uniforms came out on horses, and carriages with people in them moved across in front of the building.

Realising that the time that was left to him was short and growing ever shorter, he became exceedingly anxious that the things that he had done, the things that he had seen, and the things that he had thought and said, should be set down and recorded against the time when he would no longer be there to bear witness to them.

Others realised the way things were going, too.

An Italian journalist went out to Maralal, and, finding Kibiriti there, arranged for him to travel down to Nairobi and, for the first time in his life, to board an aeroplane, bound for London.

They took a taxi to Coulsden, where a nurse knocked at the door to Thesiger's room and led the younger man in to where he sat, in his armchair by the open window.

At first the old man could not, with his poor eyesight, make out who his visitor was.

'Wilfred,' he said, 'It is me, Kibiriti.'

'Kibiriti!' he cried. 'I would know that voice anywhere.'

He pulled himself to his feet and the two men embraced.

Kibiriti could not but notice how much older and how much weaker and more frail the old man had become.

They went out onto the lawn, Thesiger walking with two carved African sticks and Kibiriti with his arms around his shoulders to steady him.

At length the nurses came to take him back to his room.

He needed to rest, they said.

'Leave us,' he replied. 'These were my happy days.'

They stayed in the garden for most of the day.

Thesiger said that he would like to go back to Maralal to die.

'I miss it all, Kibiriti,' he said.

He remained in the home.

In the spring of 2003 he suffered a fall, after which he was confined to bed for a month, and then moved to a nursing wing where he received a greater level of care and observation.

On Sunday, 17th August, just before lunch, he fell again and, sometime later, was taken to hospital in Croydon where he was found to have fractured his femur. He was kept in hospital there for seven days, and though he was mostly conscious, he seemed, at times, to be seeing from his bed a world other than the one that others around him saw.

Of someone standing by his bed, he demanded, 'What is your tribe?'

At another time he cried out, 'For God's sake, let me go.'

On Sunday, 24th August 2003, at just after five minutes past four in the afternoon, he died.

He was ninety-three years old.

Our Dead Through Whom We Live

From the house it is a short walk to the roadside turning where the lane heads off across the land. It dips gently down, at first, between laid hedges and fields, and then it levels, crossing two bridges.

The first bridge passes over the waters of the shallow river, its wide banks grass-edged on either side.

The second, more substantial bridge, crosses a single-track railway.

The lane rises again after this, but steeply this time, so that you have to lean forwards into the slope to ascend the hillside.

At length you reach the lychgate of the small stone church of Saint Michael and All Angels, with its squat wooden bell-tower, and the path between the gravestones worn deep by the passing of generations.

'By the path of duty and sacrifice,' says the plaque at the gate, 'these passed out of sight.'

And below this the names of local men, killed in wars in foreign lands, and below these names the words.

'Our dead through whom we live.'

At this place the road ends.

From its end, three dirt tracks lead off across the hill's shoulder. One leads to the left, one to the right and a third diagonally upwards.

The upper track takes you first through a wood, the trees arching up and over and enclosing, tunnel-like; and the soft, damp earth deadening the sounds of your footsteps.

There comes a point where you leave the track and double back on yourself, joining a green path, narrower and less distinct, that leads more steeply upwards, through thickets where the trees give way to gorse and bramble that grab at you as you pass, and the rabbits, startled, scatter at your approach, and the garbled cries of pheasants taking to the air.

Then, quite suddenly you are out: out into the open air and above the treeline, on the edge of a broad expanse of rough hill-pasture, sheep-country, which you must cross before climbing again as the hill rises once more towards the ridge that marks its summit.

And the whole land is spread out around you, and the green hills and valleys surrounding.

The house is in sight once more, far below.

It was here, on this high hill, that Wilfred Thesiger's ashes were taken and scattered, above The Milebrook, his family home.

And down below, down in the valley, between the railway and the road, the River Teme meanders on its tree-lined course through fields and farms to join the River Severn in Worcestershire; and flows, from there, down to the sea.

Acknowledgements

The first thing to say is that this book would not be here without Scott Pack, who read it, liked it, published it, worked tirelessly to spread the word about it, and shared with me both tea and cakes along the way.

For my account of Wilfred Thesiger's Danakil expedition I have leant heavily on his diaries of the time, published as *The Danakil Diary: Journeys Through Abyssinia, 1930-34.* I have also drawn from his autobiography, *The Life of My Choice,* and from Michael Asher's *Thesiger.*

I am particularly indebted to Alexander Maitland's definitive, authorised biography, *Thesiger: The Life of the Great Explorer,* particularly for its account of his later years and death. Readers interested in Thesiger's life in Maralal should also consider Maitland's *Wilfred Thesiger in Africa.* More than this, Mr Maitland kindly read through the finished manuscript and offered advice and suggestions. The was above and beyond the call of duty and I am most grateful.

No account of any part of Wilfred Thesiger's life would be complete without a heartfelt plea to the reader buy, borrow or even steal his two stunningly beautiful master-works, *Arabian Sands* and *The Marsh Arabs.* I cannot recommend them highly enough.

I would also like to thank Mr Frank Gardner, himself a regular visitor to the flat in Tite Street as a young man, for buying me a cup of coffee in the BBC canteen and sparing the time to sit with me and share reminiscences.

He, like me, hadn't known who on earth Thesiger was when first he met him. The first he knew of him was when his mother caught sight of the man on a bus, and went up and invited herself and her son to tea with him.

Mum! he said, much put out, *Why do we have to go and have tea with that man? He looks like a headmaster.*

No, said his mother, *You don't understand. He's a legend.*

And indeed he was, and indeed he is.

And there was the time, years later, when Gardner filmed him for the BBC, in Dubai, in the desert, in the extreme humidity and the hundred-and-ten-degree heat, and Thesiger climbed to the top of a sand-dune, at the age of nearly ninety, in his three-piece tweed suit, and refused even to unbutton his waistcoat, still fuming from the decadence and indignity of having to travel in an air-conditioned car, which he thought an abomination.

And, later still, when he had all but lost his sight and he could no longer read, standing at the open door of his flat, and the bookcases all empty behind him.

But these are someone else's stories, and not mine.

But the point is this, I think. The point is this. Wilfred Thesiger was a man who made a difference to the world. And for those of us whose lives he touched, things will never be quite the same again.